DATE DUE

DEMCO 38-296

SILVER LININGS

Selling to the
Expanding Mature Market

Herschell Gordon Lewis

Bonus Books, Inc., Chicago

00   99   98   97   96   5   4   3   2   1

Library of Congress Cataloging-in-Publication Data

Lewis, Herschell Gordon, 1926-
    Silver linings : selling to the expanding mature market /
    Herschell Gordon Lewis.
        p.   cm.
    Includes index.
    ISBN 1-56625-058-7 (hardcover)
    1. Aged consumers—United States.   2. Marketing—United States.
    3. Advertising—United States.   I. Title.
    HC110.C6L46   1996
    658.8'348—dc20   96-21808

Bonus Books, Inc.
160 East Illinois Street
Chicago, Illinois 60611

Printed in the United States of America

Contents

Preface

The Best Is Yet to Come

The old saying, "The best is even better," could have been originated by a marketer, marveling at the skyrocketing senior citizen marketplace.

Thirty years ago, the subject of this book didn't exist.

Oh, seniors existed . . . although we called them "old people" then. It wasn't because we weren't concerned with political correctness (although we weren't). Rather, it was because we didn't consider them a separate market.

Separate? What a joke! They're far more than separate: They're the biggest niche market, and growing bigger by the hour, while other market segments are shrinking.

Some current statistics, courtesy of the marketing group Senior Ads U.S.A.:

- Seniors account for 40% of total consumer demand.
- 55% of all depositors in financial institutions are over age 55.
- 77% of all assets in the U.S.A. belong to those over age 55.
- Seniors have five times the net worth of the average American.

And that's now. The numbers leap every year and, by any expert's prognostication, will be in the upper stratosphere during the 21st century.

But 30 years ago, advertisers lionized *mass*, not *class*. The trigger words were "cost-per-thousand." Per-thousand *what*? Who cared? Television-oriented advertisers dealt in two terms that today have little relevance to the marketplace . . . although a lot of national advertisers still use them:

1. "Noted."
2. "Recall."

You recognize these as television terms. You also recognize the great flaw in both: They relate to the message, not to a positive act resulting from the message.

Today, in fact, those two words are at variance with the reaction of many seniors to advertising messages. They look with bewilderment at some of the beer commercials. They, the biggest cadre of potential customers at discount stores, look with annoyance at discount store television advertising which features odd-looking tattooed members of Generation-X, wearing baseball caps turned backward. ("Don't those caps come with instructions?" one spry elderling asked wryly.)

So, yes, advertising is becoming targeted. And no, today's "mass" advertising isn't aimed at seniors. It's unashamedly aimed at the 25–49 age group, and television shows are renewed or canceled based on their viewership within the 25-to-49ers. Nothing wrong with that, except for overlooking the demographic group with the most leisure time and the most buying power.

Today, we realize several great truths . . . truths that existed 30 years ago but weren't emphasized because most people were too polite to admit them. For example, today we know absolutely that the reader cares about three things: Me . . . myself . . . and I.

Second, we've learned a hugely valuable rule, after wasting untold billions of advertising dollars sending out expensive messages that didn't connect. That rule:

Write within the experiential background of the reader.

I'll have much to say about that rule in this book. An individual's lifetime of experiences is a comforting element to that person. And paying attention (and tribute) to the rule helps us motivate and sell.

Those two elements — the "Me, Myself, and I" recognition and the Experiential Background Rule — reflect the great change in the marketing climate. That change is *fragmentation* — the evolution of many side-by-side markets with different triggers. Mass marketing may not be the most economical way to reach the most potential buyers much longer . . . not even for items everyone uses, such as bread or margarine. It certainly isn't even now the most economical way for fund raisers to reach potential donors.

Fragmentation is a benefit for marketers who know how to pinpoint their messages. If they can pinpoint their messages and match those messages to their target prospects, they're home free.

If you want to penetrate into the core of the difference between generations, the first step is to study the circumstances under which the buying habits of each generation were established.

So we look at a huge group — the fastest-growing group of potential customers in the world — those age 50 or older. What differences do we see? What differences do we see between the 50–60 age group and the 60+ age group? And I'm not referring to physical differences, except indirectly. I'm referring to differences that enable us to reach them better with our marketing messages.

First, we have a giant change in marketing over the past two generations. Seniors began their buying history at a time when merchants knew them. The grocer knew which breakfast cereals they liked, which cuts of meat they liked, even which days were their normal shopping days. The automobile dealer knew them and their parents by name. The banker knew them on sight. None of today's computerized code numbers existed.

What am I pointing out? I'm pointing out that this is the last generation to enjoy personalized relationships with people who sold them goods and services. They not only knew their suppliers, they also knew their neighbors. And, in fact, members of a family knew each other's habits because the family met at dinner and talked; television hadn't yet eliminated the art of conversation.

What's the significance of this? Generation-X grew up with supermarkets and McDonald's and automatic teller machines. They not only don't know who lives next door to them, they don't care. They're the result of the impersonal, mass-produced, follow-whoever-is-cool MTV television generation. They expect impersonal communications and don't see any reason to be singled out as individuals. Instead, television has bred them to be comfortable with being singled out as a *group* . . . and that's not the same at all. Not at all.

But for seniors, being singled out as individuals is like going back to a comfortable home. And this explains why:

> *An impersonal communication is more likely to appear complicated than a personal communication.*

This is simple psychology. When I aim a message at *you*, you don't have any question that you're included. If I aim a message at everybody, you may wonder whether you're included. That lack of targeting has two results: First, because you have to analyze the message you're more likely to regard it as complicated. Second, because you're more likely to regard it as complicated, you're *less* likely to respond.

I have to enter a disclaimer here. I'm dealing in broad strokes, like a painter who uses a spray can instead of a camel's-hair brush. But, as chapter three points out, four different categories of seniors exist. They're all seniors. They have common traits. But each group has its own characteristics, and with each sub-group comes another packet of characteristics, some so similar they require study to understand the separation, and some radically different. So the spray-can approach covers the genre. The individual marketer covers the individual target. Otherwise, a typical chapter might be headed: "How to sell paint brushes to the 62–62½ age group."

So even as I beg your pardon for spray-painting conclusions, I *don't* apologize for spray-painting conclusions. Every marketer knows exceptions to any generic pronouncements. Exceptions don't destroy the validity; they qualify it. We deal here in procedures that should work, not in micro-circumstances the typical marketer might never face.

The point: Even as we structure our messages to *appear to be* personal, we certainly can't stop before sending each letter in a mailing of thousands of pieces or setting up a selective-bound publication ad and say, "Let's see . . . this one goes to Carl Johnson. He enjoys pizza, so we'll mention pizza in the one that goes to him. And the next letter goes to Mary Johnson. She likes to ride her bicycle, so we'll mention bicycles."

We not only can't do that in a mass mailing or a magazine ad . . . we *shouldn't* do that, because: We'd drive the cost of the communication beyond any logical limit; we couldn't possibly distribute the message in a timely manner; and if we pinpoint someone's pleasures too closely we could cause discomfort. For that matter, we could be accused of violating the person's privacy. No, we don't have to go that far, because we then would be defying logic in every manner.

So just as this book deals in broad strokes, our marketing to seniors deals in broad strokes. We may use the word "beer" and Carl Johnson will snort and say, "It should have been pizza." Okay, we won't sell to Carl Johnson. But if our message is written properly, it *will* sell to enough others to pay for itself. And that's the nature of our business — reaching and influencing the most people who can and will respond to our offer.

With that imperative in mind, let's get to work!

Herschell Gordon Lewis
Plantation, Florida, USA

(A parenthetical note: Many exhibits in this book relate directly or indirectly to AARP, the American Association of Retired People. This certainly is *not* because I either admire or abhor AARP. Rather, it's because AARP is far and away the biggest, most influential, most visible, and most prolific source of advertising materials aimed at seniors. So, naturally, AARP is similarly the biggest source of samples . . . good and bad.)

Acknowledgments

I owe a debt of gratitude to Mr. Uwe Drescher, head of Germany's leading direct response advertising agency, who gave me a professional seminar forum in Hamburg to test many of these concepts. And to Pete and Hank Hoke of *Direct Marketing Magazine*, my thanks for use of your pages to see what feedback some of these principles would bring from experienced veterans in advertising and fund raising.

But most of all — and as usual — thanks to my wife and partner Margo, for help in gathering exhibits, for encouragement, and for just being there. As Browning wrote, so perfectly it might have been just for us: *Grow old along with me! The best is yet to be.*

HGL

1

The Biggest "Niche Market"

Even as this book goes to press, the term "niche market" is obsolete, insofar as it refers to seniors. The market is too big to be relegated to niche status.

We still use niche, because "mass marketing to seniors" is increasingly both unfashionable and ineffective; but no transitional word between "mass" and "niche" has gained popular acceptance. Possibilities: "segment"; "cluster-group."

As this book will point out repeatedly, within this niche or segment or cluster-group are many sub-groups, identifiable by age (under 65 or over 65), economic circumstances (working, fixed income retired, comfortable or affluent retired), activity intensity (active or sedentary, travel-eager or travel-indifferent) . . . and these are just starters.

Reaching Seniors *As Seniors*

Fig. 1–1 is a quick example of mass marketing: a standard ad, promoting an exercise machine. We don't see the face of the model

1

(Fig. 1–1) This is a "standard" ad for an exercise machine. The model is quite deliberately chosen to appear to be any age from 20 to 50.

in the main photograph; her face appears in the smaller photo. She obviously typifies models a company would use to sell the equipment to the general marketplace — young, trim, and vigorous, the mass-market ideal.

When we run advertising aimed at seniors, the model in that first ad would actually suppress response, not enhance it. So the same advertiser, in figure 1–2a and 1–2b, uses models representing the "senior ideal" . . . not the mass-market ideal. The advertiser also knows the senior market and the value of the phrase "special senior discount," a phrase that can be pure gold when advertising to golden agers.

"Golden agers." That implies doddering Alzheimer candidates, doesn't it?

(Figs. 1–2a, 1–2b) The same exercise machine, advertised in a publication aimed at seniors, uses models with which this group more readily identifies . . . and uses appeals to which seniors have proved most likely to respond.

"Just What *Are* We Supposed to Call You?"

Let's be sure we're describing and considering the same people. Some sources call them "senior citizens"; others call them "mature adults" or, because that suggests some adults are immature, "mature persons"; yet others call them "golden agers" . . . but because people are working longer and longer and retiring later and later, the phrase "golden agers" suggests very old people. And *very* old people aren't a viable market for us. The demographic does change; from a marketing point of view, the change is recognizable and still attackable, but so insular any marketing to the *very* old has little appeal to any others.

And those considered very old in 1970 — ages 75 to 90 — now are considered "moderately old." We've seen too many pictures and videotapes of 70-year-old bungee jumpers and skydivers and scuba veterans and tennis champions to plaster a decrepit image on the group as a whole.

Of course we can simply call them all "older people"; but to someone 17 years old, the 30-somethings are older people. So, generally, in these pages, we'll call them senior citizens or seniors — people over age 55 or 60, who have buying power.

There Are These Seniors . . . and These Seniors . . . and Those Seniors

Notice the variations of a "fear" approach taken by two communications, each aimed at older people:

Fig. 1–3 has this legend on the envelope: "Over 50? Then <u>NOW</u> is the time to help avoid the big mistake* about your government benefits!" The asterisk (a weak device) brings home the threat: "It's one that can ruin your retirement!"

The technique brings response from many seniors. And it indicates a difference separating this group from other marketing targets: Fear of the future increases as age increases.

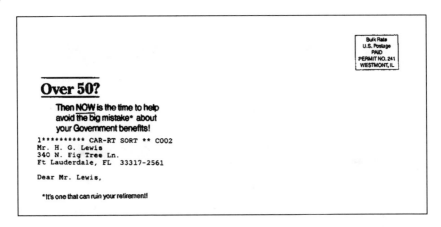

(Fig. 1–3) The purpose of the carrier envelope is to get itself opened, and that's exactly what this one will accomplish, catering to a mysterious "mistake" that could ruin retirement.

Fig. 1–4 is a mailing that intermixes fear with another effective sales weapon, special privilege. Especially forceful is "Did you now (*sic* — should be "know") that studies show SENIORS over the age of 65 will enter a nursing home or receive home health care at some point during their lifetime!!!" The three exclamation points damage the power of the message, but imagine this type of communication, properly constructed.

Another (fig. 1–5) is pure fear in action: "Over 90% of all Retired Americans will be forced to live on less than $12,000 a year." Note the emotionally-forceful subhead on this exhibit.

Interpret advertising properly, please

I want to clarify a point about the effectiveness of advertising: The difference between *looking at* something and *being reached* by something is a profound difference . . . as big a difference as the difference between the way a conventional advertiser regards a message as a success and the way a direct marketer regards a message as a success.

The conventional advertiser regards a message as a success if a reader or viewer or listener can remember it 15 minutes later. That

**IMPORTANT INFORMATION NOW AVAILABLE
GET ALL THE FACTS ON THE CHANGES IN MEDICARE**

Did you know that **MEDICARE'S** medical coverage is limited and your doctor may bill you for charges in excess of Medicare-approved limits???

Did you know that Medicare and most private **MEDICARE SUPPLEMENTS** will not pay for nursing home care or home health care.

GET ALL THE FACTS ON CATASTROPHIC CARE

Did you now that studies[1] show **SENIORS** over the age of 65 will enter a nursing home or receive home health care at some point during their lifetime!!!

Did you know that this same study[1] shows **1** out of **3** seniors will spend **3 MONTHS** or more in a nursing home and about **1** out of **4** seniors will spend **1 YEAR** or more in a **NURSING HOME???**

NOT VERY GOOD STATISTICS ARE THEY!!!

GET ALL THE FACTS ON ANNUITY ACCOUNTS

Did you know that annuity accounts offer **FLEXIBILITY, HIGH INTEREST, AND SPECIAL TAX TREATMENT???**

Did you know that annuity accounts offer penalty **FREE** withdrawals, **MEDICAID** protection and **NO PROBATE???**

Did you know that **NEW ANNUITY ACCOUNTS** offer many special features including up to an **8% BONUS** (that does not include your regular interest rate) that can be customized for your special needs??? Your old annuity accounts **CAN** and **SHOULD** be updated.

FACTS ON HOW UNCLE SAM WILL BECOME ONE OF YOUR BENEFICIARIES

Did you know **ESTATE TAXES** can cost up to **55%** of your **ESTATE???**

Learn how to **PROTECT** your hard earned **MONEY** from the grips of **ESTATE TAXES.**

**IF YOU WOULD LIKE MORE INFORMATION ON THE FACTS ABOVE,
PLEASE COMPLETE AND RETURN THE POSTAGE FREE CARD.**

PETER KEMPER AND CHRISTOPHER MURTAUGH, "LIFETIME USE OF NURSING HOME CARE," THE NEW JOURNAL OF MEDICINE 324, NO. 9
FLORIDA SENIOR PLANNERS IS NOT ASSOCIATED WITH OR ENDORSED BY MEDICARE, SOCIAL SECURITY OR ANY OTHER GOVERNMENT AGENCY

(Fig. 1–4) This primitive and typo-laden message still holds seniors' interests because it caters to their fears of being bilked. (This subject is covered more fully in chapter 5.)

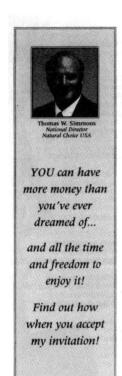

Over 90% of all Retired Americans will be forced to live on less than $12,000 a year.

SAY GOODBYE TO RESTAURANTS, VACATIONS, AND THE GOOD LIFE!

Thomas W. Simmons
National Director
Natural Choice USA

YOU can have more money than you've ever dreamed of...

and all the time and freedom to enjoy it!

Find out how when you accept my invitation!

Dear Friend,

For all the years of your life you put into making money for someone else...

For all the days and nights and weekends <u>you</u> sweated trying to make ends meet...

... this letter is for you.

WHY YOU SHOULD OWN YOUR OWN BUSINESS.

You know you'll never make any money working for someone else. If you are working for others, you're making money for <u>them</u>, but probably just scraping by yourself with <u>nothing</u> to look forward to.

**NOW YOU CAN DO SOMETHING ABOUT IT,
AND LIVE THE GOOD LIFE TODAY AS WELL AS TOMORROW.**

I have something very exciting to show you. You see, I want to introduce you to an industry where **individuals, working just a few hours a week, are making the kind of money that most people just dream about!** Let me demonstrate to you as I have to countless others that...

ONE GOOD INVESTMENT IS BETTER THAN A LIFETIME OF WORK.

I'm not kidding. This investment is, by far, one of the most amazing money–making opportunities you have ever seen. In fact, it involves all three of the hottest businesses of the past ten years: soft drinks, juices, and automatic merchandising — one of the fastest growing industries accounting for over $26–billion dollars in sales a year!

Over please...

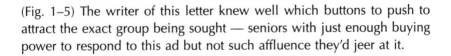

(Fig. 1–5) The writer of this letter knew well which buttons to push to attract the exact group being sought — seniors with just enough buying power to respond to this ad but not such affluence they'd jeer at it.

is what they call "recall." The genuine marketer regards a message as a success if it brings a response. That philosophy underlies many of the principles in this book, including this major one:

Getting attention is not parallel to getting response.

If we can grasp the concept that seniors prefer to be regarded as individuals, we immediately see why targeted marketing has an automatic advantage over other types of communication. Targeted marketing — *direct* marketing — by its very nature is individual, one-to-one, me-to-you. I can say to you, "I know who you are" . . . and immediately remove any resentments by saying, "I'm one too." Mass media advertising can't do that, even in vertically-targeted radio and television programs, because all the hosts of those programs can say is, "I know who you are *as a group*." And once we're in a group, the whole concept of individuality loses its strength. When anyone looks at us *as a group*, we don't think we're being regarded as individuals.

Examples, Not Statistics, Please

This knowledge, this understanding, this penetration into the core of motivations gives us another clue to effective advertising to seniors:

Statistics are cold-blooded, and cold-blooded communications are impersonal. Impersonal communications don't involve the reader. Examples are warm-blooded, and warm-blooded communications are personal. Personal communications involve the reader.

I can explain the problem caused by statistics another way. Statistics are intellectual. Examples are emotional. We have an absolute psychological rule:

When emotion and intellect come into conflict, emotion always wins. So an emotional sales argument outsells an intellectual sales argument.

This happens to be a universal truth, not limited to seniors. The difference between seniors and other age groups is what they automatically accept as emotional. This is the first generation to have daily contact with television, but many in the group did not grow up with it. Television became a marketing force in the 1950s. If I was born in the 1920s I was an adult before television became the force it is today. I wasn't dependent on television from birth, for information and as the power driving most of the images I absorbed.

Growth of TV = decline of family unit

The decline of the family as a unified group has been tied to the growth of television as the universal communicator. This has affected every one of us. No one is immune. But older people watch television as entertainment. Younger people watch television as the mirror of society. That's another reason why an impersonal television commercial has greater strength among the younger people than among the older people.

So if we use examples instead of statistics, we have a better opportunity to make a sale to a senior. An example might include a celebrity or another recognizable individual. The celebrity says, "I use it," or, "I wear it," or, "I drive it," or, "I drink it." That becomes an example.

But what if . . .

What if, instead of celebrities, to create an effective sales message to seniors we include a group of testimonials from users, with their pictures and perhaps their initials if not their names. Each of these users says, "I use it," or, "I wear it," or, "I drive it," or, "I drink it." Those, too, are examples.

Fig. 1–6 is an ad by AARP (see chapter 8). The organization, whose membership is composed entirely of seniors, wants to sell prescription drugs. Do they advertise the drugs? No. They sell *preferred position*, depending on testimonials and endorsements. The photographs are carefully chosen to represent typical seniors. The testimonials are carefully chosen to emphasize bargains, convenience, and clerks who are willing to take the time to answer all the questions seniors ask. The first quotation: "My AARP Pharmacy Service saves me $172 a year on one prescription alone."

(Fig. 1–6) The carefully-chosen cross-section of seniors and the testimonials, each underscoring a different sales point, combine to make this an effective advertisement.

You can see how a reader will respond to this next message: "I almost trashed the booklet that ended my crippling pain!" (Fig. 1–7). This is a user . . . obviously a senior. Notice that he's dressed in farm clothes. The purpose is to point out: He still is very active.

Read his testimonial: "Eight months ago, my hands hurt so bad, I couldn't even put my billfold in my back pocket. Today, when I feel up to it — I'm able to work 12 to 14 hour days on my farm."

Notice that he's identified as being 85 years old. If the advertiser had chosen someone 55 years old, the endorsement would have been considerably weaker.

But to say, as some advertising does, "78% of all users showed relief from arthritis pain" . . . that's a report, not a sales talk. We might accept the report, but not on an emotional level. It's the difference between a reporter's account in the newspaper and an editorial in the newspaper. Or perhaps the comic strip.

(Chapter 2 explores the difference between statistics and examples from another perspective.)

"I Almost Trashed the Booklet That Ended My Crippling PAIN!"

Eight months ago, my hands hurt so bad, I couldn't even put my billfold in my back pocket! Today, when I feel up to it—I'm able to work 12 to 14 hour days on my farm."

—*Donald R. Florea, 85 year old retired farmer, real estate broker, and father of fifteen.*

"...and would have lost the relief that 64,261 former sufferers now enjoy!"

Dear Friend: My name is Donald R. Florea and I thank God that I'm pain-free at 85. I also thank God that Eugene Rausch shared his experience in using *Catherine's Choice Aloe Vera Capsules*. And I *know* it was an act of God that placed the booklet with Eugene's message of relief in my hands. *You see...*

"I Nearly Threw My Salvation in the Garbage!"

I receive 5 to 10 pieces of mail every day, and Eugene's booklet was not addressed to me but was placed in my mailbox by mistake. I never read "junk" mail so I threw it out. But, as it was lying there in the trash—this statement caught my eye. It read:

How a Desperate 84-Year Old Man Went from UNBEARABLE PAIN to BLISSFUL RELIEF!

Being 85 myself and in intense pain, something told me to "PICK IT UP AND READ IT!" I read that Eugene Rausch at 84 suffered from four types of headache pain all at once. He had terrible migraines since he was six. Then surgery left him with two new and different headaches. Still another type of headache resulted from stress. All the doctors could do was prescribe pain pills.

1

(Fig. 1–7) This near-perfect message is a first-person narrative in a 16-page self-mailer. Although the reversed legend over the photograph is too small to be read easily by many seniors, those who do read it will read on eagerly because of the late revelation — the writer is 85 years old.

Emotion over intellect

How does this knowledge that emotion outsells intellect translate itself into a formula we can use every day, when we market to seniors?

The very easy formula:

Emotion outsells intellect . . . benefits are more emotional than features . . . so benefits outsell features.

I certainly hope you're saying, "Of course that's true." If you say that, you understand human psychology. And an understanding of human psychology is the nucleus of an ability to reach and influence any particular group.

A study of geese showed the typical goose has its psychological profile set in just two hours. Two hours! When that goose is two hours old, from that moment it forever will be aggressive, fighting its way to the front of the feeding trough . . . or it will hang back, forever being timid and meek. In two hours the personality of that goose is established forever.

For a human being the process takes about 40 years, but by that time our brains have hardened into cement. Try to insert a new idea and something cracks. It may be the brain; it also may be the new idea.

Resistance to Change:
How to Capitalize on It

The older we get, the less receptive we are to new ideas. And knowing this fact is a weapon for the marketer. We have a rule — and we actually can use the rule to help us sell:

The older we get, the more we resist change.

The older we get, the more likely we are to say, "That isn't the way I do it" or we say, "I've always done it this way" or "I use this brand" or "I don't understand why you changed this." The older we get, the more *inflexible* we are.

I know writers — writers, for heaven's sake! — who refuse to learn how to use a computer. Guess what age bracket these writers are in. Some still write on yellow notebook paper. They say, "I've always done it this way." (See chapter 5 for more horror stories such as this.)

Are any of these writers under age 40? Of course not.

We get stubborn. We cling to the old ideas the way a baby clings to its blanket. And more and more, as we age we fall victim to another psychological maxim:

It is easier to renounce the obvious than it is to renounce the traditional.

The reason should be clear: To be traditional, an action has to transpire over a period of time. Young people haven't lived long enough to be trapped in their traditions. A tradition of two years isn't really a tradition; it's a habit. A tradition of 30 or 40 years is — well, believe me, it's a tradition.

Remember when the communications giant, AT&T, split into many companies? And remember when not just MCI and Sprint but dozens of other companies moved into long distance services, driving the cost down . . . as competition always does?

Remember when AT&T moved back into local service, competing with its natural children, again driving down the price and by offering incentives forcing others to offer incentives?

Remember when cable companies only offered cable TV and not phone service and Internet access? Remember when the Internet wasn't a competitor for advertising dollars?

The invasion of cable TV companies into phone service and the eruption of the Internet as an advertising medium shook up the world of advertising. Which group was both *least* and *last* affected? Seniors.

When AT&T broke its local service into many "Baby Bells" and began fighting to hold its share of long distance services, the company had to fight to hold its customers against a barrage of advertising by MCI and Sprint. Which group stayed with AT&T in the biggest numbers?

Of course: Seniors. Seniors resist change. "The obvious" was a lower price from MCI and Sprint. "The traditional" was the comfort they felt with AT&T. It's easier to renounce the obvious than to renounce the traditional. Knowing this works two ways for the marketer arrowing messages at seniors:

What a newcomer should do, to appeal to seniors, is to avoid the appearance of newness.

Please understand: This concept does *not* refer to newness of product within a line, unless that newness is incomprehensible to seniors. The reference is to the company itself. Even the company name should sound traditional.

As this book will describe elsewhere, when we sell camcorders and videocassette recorders and computers and software, we have to be careful to match our messages to our targets. Do they nod sagely, then leave, totally unaware of what we were talking about because we used even a single word that threw them off track?

And that's why some marketers carefully establish three separate images: One of deliberate newness for those in the age 20 to 35 bracket; one of tradition for the seniors; and a third, straight-ahead image for those age 35 to 60, the group most likely to be in a position to make a change in habits and patterns. This third image, properly advertised, leaks over into the other two groups and makes the change more acceptable.

Follow this bit of information to its proper conclusion:

Resistance to change and a conservative point of view go together.

Resistance to change and a conservative point of view are more than cousins: They're brothers . . . almost *twin* brothers.

(Does this make the high percentage of seniors who vote Democratic an anomaly? Not at all, because another factor overrides all else: Social Security, the uneasy assurance of at least a minimally-comfortable future. The image of Democrats is preservation of this program; the image of Republicans is diminution of it.)

How does this information help us when we market to seniors? First of all, we don't approach them with the suggestion that we're going to change a pattern that has given them comfort. Instead, we tell them we'll help them *improve* that pattern.

Major and Minor Motivators

Envy is a peculiar motivator. Young people have been known to kill because of envy, but seniors aren't likely to buy because of it. As one ages, murder decreases but bitterness increases. If you build a sales campaign around envy you might be costing yourself response, because seniors are sensitive to being accused of being envious.

But they are. We solve the problem by suggesting exclusivity, which implies that others will be envious of us. Exclusivity works. And of the five major motivators of the late 1990s — *fear, guilt, greed, need for approval,* and *exclusivity* — exclusivity is by far the easiest to create.

Just follow a pattern which says to the reader: "Everybody wants it . . . nobody can get it . . . except you." Or, "Only you . . . only from us." As an extra thought: Whenever you put together a marketing message based on exclusivity, be sure to include an expiration date. Including an expiration date increases response. Chapter 3 expands on this point.

Three little words; one giant word

Let's move a little deeper into the psychology of selling to older people.

Three little words can be the difference between reader comfort and reader antagonism: "We both know." We and the reader are partners. And partners have that wonderful relationship that can make a gigantic difference in selling *anything* to *anyone.* That relationship is:

Rapport.

I'm your friend, not some unknown salesman trying to change you against your will.

Now we've established rapport. How do we use that rapport?

We know seniors are conservative. We know they resist change. So we avoid the suggestion of change as much as we can.

If we're selling them an electronic device we tell them, "You can handle this easily, and your lifestyle will be more comfortable." We don't suggest a long learning process. We don't suggest that their lifestyle will be disrupted.

If we're selling them pharmaceuticals — and this is a giant field for seniors — we tell them they will feel better and even recover some lost powers. You may think it's strange, but to this group recovering lost powers sells better than achieving new powers. That isn't true of younger people. If you want to increase response by a huge amount, suggest this recovery of lost powers is something they can do themselves, without having to visit a doctor or a therapist.

Fig. 1–8 is a "restoration" ad — "Bring Back the Pleasure of Reading." The aim is clear: those who have quit reading conventional books because eyesight isn't strong enough to read comfortably.

If we sell entertainment or education, we don't suggest work. Never work. Everything is easy. Everything is pleasant. Everything will make them more desirable, better conversationalists, superior to others who just sit there, stuck in the past. It's actually a paradox: We tell them they won't be sitting in the past, and we do it carefully so they won't realize we're trying to get them out of their past habits and traditions.

Don't damage the fragile rapport

Some of the methods we use in the general marketplace to unlock reluctance work very poorly on seniors. If we say, "Act now!" or "Urgent!" without adding proof of value for such an action, we can damage response because we damage rapport.

Rapport drives our messages. Rapport stems from a relationship, not from product. So unless you specifically want to avoid reader involvement in your message, always write in the active voice. If you're referring to investments, write, "We will examine

Bring Back the Pleasure of Reading
with Large Print Books from Random House

LARGE PRINT EDITION
LAUREN BACALL
NOW

LARGE PRINT EDITION
DEAN KOONTZ

LARGE PRINT EDITION
James A. Michener
RECESSIONAL

DARK RIVERS OF THE HEART

Random House Large Print Editions
Available at your local bookstore. To receive a brochure of Random House Large Print titles call 800-793-2665

(Fig. 1–8) This ad makes great sense to some, no sense to others. It's a directly targeted ad, but even so, it might succeed in the book section of a general circulation newspaper . . . because those who read the book section may be the ideal targets.

your portfolio," *not* "Your portfolio will be examined." If you're offering medical services, write, "I really think this will be beneficial for you," not, "This will be to your benefit."

Rapport blooms like a flower when active voice ties you and your senior target together. It wilts like a flower when passive voice keeps you separated.

You can see for yourself. What is the difference between:

1. "Your books will be sent to you."
2. "We'll send your books to you."

In the first instance we deny a relationship. In the second instance, we claim a relationship. Which statement has greater rapport?

Rapport serves another purpose: When you put a friendly arm around the shoulder of an uncertain prospect . . . and when your prospect recognizes the arm around his or her shoulder as a friendly one and not one aimed at the pocketbook . . . that individual becomes more likely to accept change, because you're right there with him or her. Acceptance of change is one of the most difficult challenges marketers face in selling to this group.

Basic Psychology

To meet and conquer that challenge, the marketer should have a basic knowledge, a primitive knowledge, of psychology . . . some idea of how to lead the targets to change without having them feel angry or resentful.

An example of how we can do this is the difference between the standard question, "Isn't this what you want?" and the leading question, "This is what you want, isn't it?" The second question leads the reader and includes the possibility of the reader saying yes. Without those last words — "isn't it?" — we have a command, and seniors positively will resist a command. With those last words — "isn't it?" — we appear to be performing a service.

And beyond performing a service, we direct the thought without being dictatorial. Commands work poorest on our best targets. Those who are most likely to follow an outright command are those who have the least buying power. So we don't command. Instead, we direct the thought.

(Actually, we *are* commanding, but the reader thinks he or she has reached a conclusion. At least, that's our intention.)

So ask yourself: What is the difference between . . .

Do you want to live to be 100?

and . . .

Don't you want to live to be 100?

Each suggests a different challenge. If you ask someone, "Do you want to live to be 100?" you risk a "No, I don't" answer . . . but you also might benefit from a positive answer which begins a dialogue.

That response differs from the one you'll get when you ask, "*Don't* you want to live to be 100?" You say to the reader, "I expect a 'Yes' answer, and if you don't answer 'Yes,' you're a fool." Usually this is stronger as a response motivator than "Do you want to live to be 100?" . . . but you can see circumstances in which the assumption is dangerous and you'd be both safer and more likely to generate a response by using "Do" instead of "Don't."

(If this whole point confuses you, just use "Don't" and forget about the comparison.)

A Potpourri of Suggestions

Here's an example of how we can lead the reader by the hand and cause that reader to form a conclusion. The reader *thinks* he or she has formed the conclusion independently. We know better, because we've led that reader by the hand. We made the choice, by our use of words:

Singular suggests *exclusivity*; collective nouns suggest *universality*. For example:

1. "You'll save on anything you see in these pages."
2. "You'll save on everything you see in these pages."

What do we want the reader to think? "Anything" is singular. It isolates without specifying. It says to the reader, "Choose what you want and enjoy a discount." "Everything" is a collective noun, saying, "Whatever you want from these pages is yours at a discount." Does "everything" generate more response than "anything"? In this use, yes. But if I say to you, "Order *anything* and I'll ship it to you within 24 hours," that is stronger than saying, "I'll send you everything you order within 24 hours." We're in command, and our job as professional marketers is to structure messages that work for us with maximum power.

Some of these points may appear to be subtle. They aren't at all subtle. To a senior, aware of a wolf pack hunting his or her money, we have to appear to be neutral even as we guide the decision-making process. This is *not* easy . . . but it certainly can be worthwhile, because seniors are sensitive to correctness.

Sensitivity to correctness dictates another difference in marketing to seniors: We should be somewhat more formal than we'd be with younger markets. The trend, worldwide, is toward informality. But trends filter upward, not downward, and the last group to accept informality . . . *except* from someone they accept as a member of their own group . . . is the senior cadre. If you aren't one too and aren't able to identify yourself as a senior, stay away from informality on your first contact by mail or phone. (This concept as it applies to telemarketing is covered in chapter 9.)

Prove Your Claim

This leads us to a logical extension of the sales technique we should use when advertising to seniors. Seniors resist change. They want to be comfortable when they make a decision. So give them comfort by proving your claim.

Prove your claim. The younger an individual is, the less proof he or she demands. That's why so many countries have severe rules about advertising to children. Children believe what you tell them. They acquire layers of skepticism as they age, but those layers of skepticism aren't there when they're very young. Skepticism is the result of disappointments, and it takes a few years to pile up enough disappointments to make someone skeptical. So the younger we are, the more accepting we are.

But seniors — they've had year after year to see claims destroyed. They've had year after year to see their beliefs dashed on the hard rocks of reality. They've had year after year to realize that what they thought was true was just another piece of advertising "puffery." If they conclude you're just another member of the wolf pack whose only interest is to take their money and run away with it, you have no chance of making a sale.

Prove your claim. This is where endorsements and testimonials have value. This is where the wording of your mailing or your advertisement has to be clear and straightforward.

This may seem to contradict a previous point: A circus-like layout, with big bold type and lots of colors, can break through the barrier of apathy. Seniors may not have seen everything on this planet, but many of them *think* they've seen everything . . . and if we don't get their attention we lose the battle before the first shot is fired.

If you decide to use a big, bold layout, use words such as "Guarantee" and "Positive Proof" and "Here is the evidence you have been waiting for." This combines attention-getting with words that bring comfort and overcome the automatic skepticism.

Conclusion

If you want to condense this introductory chapter into one single sentence, this would be the sentence:

Tell people what they want to hear or read, not what you want to say.

I know this is difficult. I know that we, as marketers, are just as thoroughly infected by the "Me-myself-I" syndrome as the people to whom we are advertising. But if you keep score by the number of times the telephone and cash register ring, this condensed warning should be one you paste on your keyboard . . . or better yet, on your brain. If you're trying to sell to me, I don't care what it is. I care about what it will do for me. Tell people what they want to hear and read, not what you want to say.

The fastest-growing group of targets are old fogeys, old worn-out hulks (like me) — people who are in a race to see which will come first: Will their hair turn completely white or fall out?

Between now and the year 2010 first-world countries will see a one and a half percent *drop* in the number of people under age 50 and a 76 percent increase in the number of people over age 50. So knowing how to sell to seniors can give you a very profitable competitive edge.

But please remember what Alexandre Dumas said so many years ago: "All generalizations are false, including this one." Seniors have one thing in common: age. Beyond that, we marketers will continue to fight fragmentation. If we keep our wits about us and if we continue to test, test, test, we won't see handwriting on the wall. Instead, that handwriting will be on checks made out to us, signed by seniors we somehow have convinced will benefit from what we sell to them. And seeing those checks coming in to our offices will keep us forever young.

2

How Seniors Differ
(or Do They?)

Physically, no question.

The face sags. The breasts droop. The prostate balloons. The veins turn visible. The fingers gnarl. The nails thicken. The hair thins. The eyelids droop. The hearing decays.

Not much of a listing, is it . . . especially since procedures exist for masking or correcting every one of those degenerative changes?

So is the over-50 group really different from their under-50 soon-to-be-replacements?

The answer parallels a venerable joke about the fellow who had a date with a pair of Siamese twins. The next day his friend asked, "Did you have a good time?" His answer: "Well, yes and no."

Two Marketplaces. Two Targets?

Marketers often mistakenly lump two groups together. Anyone over age 50 becomes a nodule on a lump, the "Senior Market" category.

The previous paragraph has two words worthy of analysis, not just one. The first is "often" . . . because "often" isn't "always." If what you're selling deals with health or insurance or investments, the senior market does have *some* singular characteristics that demand singular attention.

The second word is "mistakenly" . . . because lumping those groups together is a mistake only when marketing a product or service whose efficacy changes when the individual's posture in the work force changes or dissolves.

The astute marketer recognizes retiring from the work force as a *major* lifestyle change; becoming age 51 or age 65 is a *minor* lifestyle change.

Oh, certainly, moving into a Medicare age eliminates an individual as a target for primary health insurance; but that same individual becomes a far more receptive target for supplementary coverage.

Television for decades maintained a dogged insistence on the 25–49 age group as the only logical targets. The enduring success of programs with a geriatric protagonist, such as the long-running *Murder, She Wrote* . . . or the hard-edged news commentary *20/20* whose hosts were both "seniors" . . . did little to dislodge this premise. Only when advertisers analyzed their own responses did attitudes begin to change.

(1996 was considered a pivotal year because this was the year the "baby boomers" began to turn 50. The publication *USA Today* reported that in the year 1996 a baby boomer turned 50 every 8.4 seconds, anticipating a speedup to every 6.8 seconds by 2001.)

Obviously, selective marketing makes sense where it is practical. In mass media, where it is less practical, a better dividing line is 65, not 50 . . . and that number creeps ever upward, so 70 might be a better border. A major exception: Offering a premium or benefit to *any* group will increase response. Thus, including the 50+ group with the 65+ group in a "Special Shopping Day" or "Senior Discount" will increase response. That same 51-year-old who deeply resents being regarded as beyond early middle age will happily trot into the senior arena to collect a bonus . . . then trot back to an earlier-age niche.

Differences *do* exist, not only within the polyglot 50+ group but between the under-50s and the over-50s. Recognizing the gospel of the statement "All generalities are false, including this one," let's take a shot at some of those differences.

Creeping Subjectivity

As people age, they become more subjective. "What does this mean to *me*?" becomes a standard question about news, about politics, and about advertising.

So *relevance* is a master key, and the key opens the lock with greater and greater ease as age progresses.

Why? One reason is, regrettably, the gradual narrowing of the range of interests. "I like this and I don't like that" loses its solidity as one emerges from infancy into the flowering world of adulthood . . . then hardens again as one slides into a less-elastic elderly universe.

Some years ago, when then-President George Bush announced that he wasn't going to eat broccoli because he'd earned the right to dislike broccoli, he wasn't just exhibiting a semi-humorous petulance and lack of nutritional information; he was typifying an attitude: *I've worked all my life to do what I want to do.* Experimentation? What for? Who has time? It *might* taste good or look good or smell good or feel good . . . but it also might not. Why should I take a chance?

Marketers who recognize this can take advantage of the *touchstone* technique of salesmanship — tying what they're selling to a known and accepted base.

The touchstone overcomes a common marketing problem: You want to make a claim, but you don't have sufficient facts to implement the claim. So you tie your claim to a touchstone:

— *What if you had been able to buy Microsoft stock at issue, in 1981? Some investors did.*

— *My mirror shows me the same youthful face it showed me thirty years ago. Yours can too.*

— *Think of the most exciting golf hole you've ever played. Now multiply by ten!*

The touchstone prevents *evaluation* of the claim. And critical evaluation is the bane of advertising to seniors, because these targets have the time and the background to evaluate.

Testimonials are touchstones. For seniors, three types of testimonials add a façade of *objectivity*, masking and obscuring their subjectivity:

1. Peer testimonials. "Mature" resorts, communities, and condominia use prototypical models or buyers.
2. Group testimonials. A batch of names, complete with city and state, is a powerful touchstone.
3. Celebrity testimonials. These are the least dependable, because the very nature of subjectivity includes formation of black-or-white images of celebrities. Some are obvious: Rock stars (were an advertiser to seniors unwise enough to use one of them) would suppress response, not enhance it. Country-and-western singers are venerated by some, bewildering to some, and detested as lower-caste by some. Television stars may be totally unknown to those who keep their sets tuned to a single channel day and night.

Tip: Two easy ways of implementing a touchstone for almost any product or service:

1. "If you liked that, you'll love this."
2. "Remember how great *[WHATEVER]* used to be? Now that pleasure is yours again, even better than before."

Who Says Nostalgia Ain't What It Used to Be?

Strangers in a strange land. That's how many seniors feel, hearing popular music that isn't popular music, watching in bewilderment as movie and television stars they don't recognize are lionized and mobbed by fans, feeling left behind as the Internet deposits terms such as "URL" and "Hyperlink" onto their unwitting consciousness.

So their own hyperlink — nostalgia — can be exploited profitably. The link with the known past is infinitely more comfortable than a link with the uncertain future. Ads such as fig. 2–1a through 2–1e are aimed squarely at those to whom rap stars and computer geeks are symbols of their "out of it" non-status. "Remember

(Figs. 2–1a — 2–1e) These ads for music of a bygone era have seniors humming the tunes and wondering, "Why don't they play music like that any more?" Many newspapers now carry Question-and-Answer columns: "Where can I find a recording of this old tune?"

(Fig. 2–2) Younger folk probably have no idea what a soapstone stove is. To an elderly person with buying power, it's a link to a happy past.

when . . ." is a stalwart touchstone sales aid when appealing to those who have buying power but little identification with contemporary cultural, political, social, or even religious philosophies.

Who would want an old soapstone stove? For some seniors, displaying this piece of furniture is a comforting link to the past. Fig. 2–2 would have little appeal to the under-50s.

This isn't to say the seniors are the ones who are out of step. History may prove exactly the opposite. But marketers are only parenthetically fashioners of society; in their primary function, they're the mirrors of it.

Implicit Skepticism and How to Handle It

Envision a group of five-year-olds watching television. See their eyes shine as an especially adept commercial grabs and shakes their imaginations? They believe. They haven't amassed the educational and perceptual base that sifts through claims and rejects those lacking credence within their experiential background. That's why laws

(Fig. 2–3) Note the first sentence of selling text: "How long has it been since you last enjoyed the soft ticking sound of a finely made watch?" The emphasis on Russian manufacture may damage response, because the memory is of railroad watches; but the image is unmistakable: The head nods, yes, that was a kinder, gentler time.

exist, protecting children from exaggerated advertising claims.

Now envision a group of 65-year-olds watching television. Each commercial warrants a wisecrack or a shake of the head or a statement of disbelief . . . or the dispassionate statement, "That was a clever commercial," the very remark categorizing the commercial as non-involving; and dovetailing it rather than allowing it to penetrate.

This is one reason advertisers who depend on hyperbole feel their advertising can reach and influence powerfully, within the 50+ group, only those with the least amount of buying power. They're only partially right, of course; but the logic is that the lower down the economic scale a target individual is, the less likely he or she is to have the osmotic effect of acceptance seeping out and analysis seeping in. This same psychology drives those advertising sweepstakes and lotto programs: Hopes and dreams are the "live" escape mechanisms.

But a counter-mechanism exists, combating skepticism: The "I'm Entitled to Special Benefits" Syndrome.

So the advertiser who leans heavily on *exclusivity* — "Only you get this gigantic discount or free offer or opportunity" — has a major edge. The one governor on the throttle: credibility.

Testimonials, mentioned in the previous section of this chapter, are excellent devices for dispelling skepticism. The careful marketer precedes negotiation with a celebrity with surveys of groups representative of those he/she wants to attract. Some nasty surprises await marketers who invest in a celebrity and build a campaign around a personality rejected by a majority of the target group.

Here are some "public domain" phrases designed to overcome skepticism. Worked into advertising or direct mail copy, they have a huge psychological edge over standard claims of superiority or usefulness:

- "Here's proof:"
- "Folks like you said this:"
- "We wouldn't offer you a 100% guarantee if we weren't 100% sure."
- "Believe it or not:"
- "An independent report:"

You've noticed that most of these end with a colon, not a period. That's quite on purpose, a rhetorical trick: As the colon preceding this statement shows, this punctuation mark demands *ongoing* reading because it says to the reader, "What follows explains, justifies, and proves."

To sell them, tell them: "You're *right* to be skeptical!"

A truism? Not quite, but it's close: Seniors who are most able to buy what you have to sell are those who most demand that you agree with them.

If you're puzzling over that statement, recognize its worth to a marketer trying to crash through a steel-reinforced concrete barrier

— the What-does-this-mean-to-me? attitude reinforced by skepticism, the natural parent of many negative marketing experiences.

So a magalog with the title "The Great Retirement Betrayal" (fig. 2–4) has an automatic competitive edge as it enters the arena:

(Fig. 2–4) This cover of a "magalog" — a mailing for a retirement newsletter, cast as a magazine — uses a caricature of the famous Grant Wood painting as the background for powerful selling copy. Note the "For sale by owner" sign on the house.

It says to the recipient, "See? You're right!" Automatically, the image of the mailing is elevated from "another piece of mail" to a friend who knows what he's talking about.

Naked stroking? If so, so what? Here we have salesmanship in action, tailored to the group at which it's aimed instead of the more typical, "Here's how we sell to anybody."

Compare what appears to be an exposé with the standard "You've earned it" copy we so often (and so desperately) fling at the mature marketplace. No contest, for this type of intensive and argumentative selling.

But "You've earned it" has some potent psychological seeds in it. Figs. 2–5 and 2–6 may be transparent to some. Fine: Those aren't the ones who will respond. Others will.

No, this conclusion is not the suggestion that every mailing to seniors masquerade as an exposé. The point is more profound and

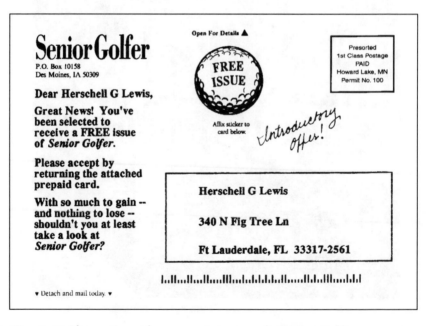

(Fig. 2–5) The notion of a magazine named *Senior Golfer* may seem bizarre: Do seniors play a different game? But, as is true of any chosen selling approach, some will respond to the "Great News! You've been selected . . ." theme.

(Fig. 2–6) "You've earned it" isn't always credible. But to some, heads will nod, yes, I've earned it.

applies to all market segments, not just the over-50s or over-65s: Saying "I agree with you" is *not* as strong as having *your target* say "I agree with you." You can generate that result only by knowing in advance what that target individual wants to read or hear.

Don't Over-promote

Wait a moment: Is it *possible* to over-promote to seniors?

Good question. If you're operating inside the recipient's experiential background, telling him/her what he/she wants to hear, then *no* . . . it's darned near impossible to over-promote.

The Rule:

If your message reinforces a pre-existing attitude, then repetition is not redundant and introduction of parallel evidence is not oversell. The only qualifier is the standard qualifier of all salesmanship: When your prospect says yes, stop selling. And stop explaining.

If you're introducing a new product or service and you can't figure out a way to coattail-ride on an existing prejudice, then *yes*, you can over-promote.

If you're using as spokespersons individuals with whom your typical target can't or won't identify, then *yes*, you can over-promote.

If you're suggesting that young people have an automatic edge over older people and pitch this theme mercilessly, then *yes*, you can over-promote.

So the intensity of your advertising message should be geared to your ability to tie it to a cemented prejudice.

Here's the paradox:

Children have automatic prejudices: "I love this. I hate that." Their likes and dislikes change as fast as a box of cereal offers a different toy.

Let's insert a parenthetical marketing injunction: The word "you" *can* be overused, and here are two ways in which unaware marketers overuse the word:

1. A too-early assumption that the sale has been made can result in the sale being lost. Saying *"your* new car" or *"your* lovely dress" too early in the copy can trigger a senior's automatic response: "I'm making up my own mind." A plastic attitude begins too harden too soon. "I'm not saying 'no'" becomes "I'm not saying 'yes' and I'm not saying 'no'" — which means "no."
2. Use of the word *you* decreases in value proportionately to an increase in upscale image. This is because the aura of exclusivity gives way to the feeling, "I'm being pitched."

Does this mean the road to riches, marketing to seniors, isn't paved with gold after all?

Heck, no. It just means a marketer has to both recognize *and apply* the rules of marketing psychology.

That obviously also pertains in an appeal to a preconceived prejudice. Powerful stuff, this!

Fig. 2–7 hits home hard. One of the best sales pitches to

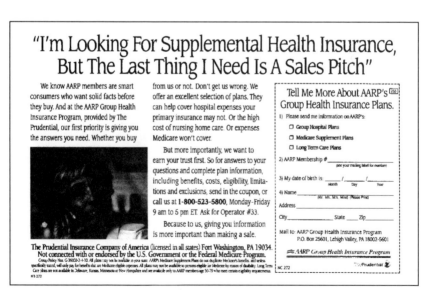

(Fig. 2–7) Clever wording! Most people *aren't* looking for supplemental health insurance, but the second line of the heading causes them to read — and perhaps respond to — this ad.

seniors is an attack on sales pitches. The promise "we want to earn your trust" won't ring hollow to those who have become disgusted with high-pressure salespeople.

Conclusion

As individuals age, they temper their prejudices, either through recognition of social niceties, education, mellowing personal experiences, or changes in their personal circumstances. Then, as they age further, the tempering begins to thin, and prejudices harden once again. This is why lawyers, questioning potential jurors, are especially careful when trying to ferret out a senior's hidden bias.

And it's why smart marketers cater to what exists . . . instead of trying to change it.

3

The Four Categories —
Similarities and Differences

Many marketers recognize only two categories of seniors — those who still are working and those who no longer are working.

That's "Depression Era" thinking. As we roll toward the 21st century, four different senior categories are worthy of attention as separate marketing targets. In ascending order, based on the most logical means of gauging their worth to us as marketers — buying power:

- Fixed income;
- Comfortable;
- Still working;
- Affluent.

Obviously, overlap exists. Many "still working" are affluent. But we aren't describing absolutes; we're describing an attitudinal receptivity or rejection in which an appeal to the wrong category can destroy the effectiveness of a marketing campaign.

(A fifth category exists — "Non-Self-Supporting" — but this category is of little value in marketing because of minimal buying power. Some advertisers of staples, such as bread, milk, beer, and in fact the lotteries, include this category by avoiding any economic status in their appeals; but no major marketer mounts an appeal directly to this group.)

Fixed Income

The fixed income group is not only huge; it's the most easily identified segment because members of this group are almost 100 percent retired, or, because of disability, out of the working force. Income isn't necessarily tiny, because many retirees have pensions in addition to Social Security . . . and within this same group, many augment both pension and their monthly Social Security checks by part-time or clandestine work.

But the buying position is universal. The standard reaction, one advertisers should recognize:

Caution.

"I'm on a fixed income" is a battle cry . . . a negative battle cry, used as a bastion against advertising that seems overly promotional. To reach members of this group, the message should be cloaked in sweet reason.

The letter shown in Fig. 3–1 is just such an appeal — "Don't let them take it away, because if they do you're in trouble."

One factor to be considered is the high percentage of former union members in this group. The union mind-set differs substantially from the entrepreneurial mind-set. Union members are used to making demands and, if necessary, making sacrifices to force those demands to be met. So if these individuals are your targets, a "Don't let them take away what you've worked so hard to get" approach is totally valid.

Oddly, those on fixed incomes are the same individuals most likely to succumb to borderline or downright illegal telemarketing sales pitches. This undoubtedly is because, observing others who either have climbed out of this category or never been part of it, a retiree sees a chance to escape from the stringent world of penny-pinching.

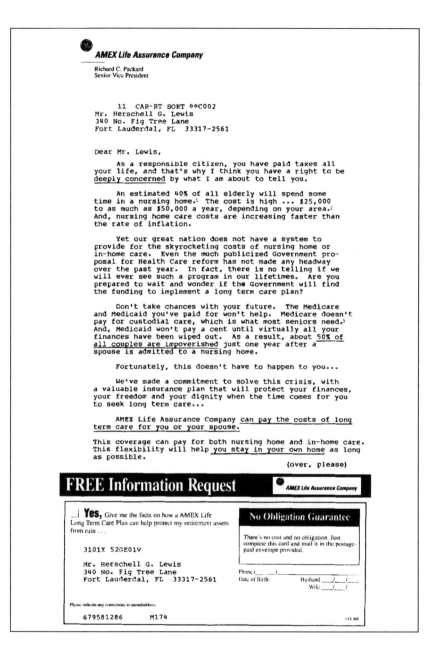

(Fig. 3–1) Those on fixed incomes will identify with this message. "Don't take chances with your future" hits home hard. (Suggestion for improvement: The numerical footnote indications are out of key with the dynamic aspect of this letter.)

This same syndrome underlies the gigantic fixed-income participation in lotteries, in nickel and quarter slot machine activity in Las Vegas and Atlantic City, and in low-stakes bingo games.

Comfortable

The "comfortable" group is the one at whom most marketers prefer to aim, not only because discretionary buying power is present but also because the age range is considerably broader. Few seniors living on a fixed income, other than ex-military personnel, are under age 62; many seniors living in comfortable circumstances are between 55 and 62.

The common-denominator approach to the comfortable group is a variation of "You've earned it," described in the previous chapter. The variation: "Because you are who you are, this is for you. (Example: Figs. 3–2 and 3–3.)

The people at whom we aim these messages have a feeling of accomplishment which, most veteran marketers conclude, can't be over-massaged.

Because this group enjoys a modicum of comfort, status is also a potent appeal. Exclusivity, the easiest-to-mount of the great motivators, works well when aimed at an individual or family of moderate affluence.

Note, please, that "family" usually means husband and wife, children having flown the nest. (Appeals to seniors as grandparents are discussed in the next chapter.)

Of all seniors, this category is the one most likely to include aggressive status-seekers. This makes them ideal for offers of *displayables* such as collector's plates and music boxes, coffee-table books, and wall accessories.

Comfortables are the best group of targets for what might be called "better living upgrade." So advertising for a Florida home or for exercise equipment, for example — upgrade options — is well-aimed at those who live comfortably. Fig. 3–4 masks its intent — selling homes — by apparently being a vacation offer. The photograph matches the "comfortables" — the ones the advertiser is after.

(Fig. 3–2) Note the "upgrade" wording — "Enjoy a Florida *Millionaire* Lifestyle. . . ." Those on fixed incomes are very much aware of social stratification. This advertiser cleverly plays to that awareness.

Opinions are mixed about the motivators to be used in financial or investment advertising. One widely-held concept is that because these people don't want any threats to their comfort, investments should be pitched on the twin bases of *safety* and *assured return*.

(Fig. 3–3) "Everything and more, for much less than we expected" has a dual appeal: It caters both to seniors' desire to get the most for their money and their desire to enjoy the lifestyle they feel they deserve.

(Fig. 3–4) Seniors in the "comfortable" category will recognize themselves in this photograph. Recognition then generates response.

Not as widely held but having the ability to generate response from those who think their investments already provide safety and assured return is "golden speculation." This type of advertising — dangerous and exotic, and therefore carrying the seeds of big success or big failure — tells the reader, "You're ready for a big win and you have time to enjoy it." Typically, the advertising doesn't feature the mechanics of the investment but, rather, the hoped-for eventual fruits of this move — travel, a luxury car, the same elements we find in sweepstakes promotions.

Still Working

Those who are still working defy a single demographic definition. Some are still working because they must; either they have obligations beyond any retirement or Social Security benefits, or they aren't entitled to such benefits.

Others are still working because they enjoy their jobs and are in a work environment that doesn't demand mandatory retirement. Their lifestyle still is seamless, and they are the group least likely to acknowledge a change of age plateau.

Others have reached executive status and enjoy a professional position which bestows both authority and power. They are loath to relinquish this position even though they would be well above the survival line if they retired.

Awareness of the future — "Where will you be five years from now?" or "What the future can hold for you" — can penetrate all levels of the still-working category. Obviously, the lower or higher this approach is pitched, the more it excludes those who conclude (rationally or irrationally), "This doesn't apply to me."

Note the difference between "What the future can hold for you" and "What does the future hold for you?" These are in no way parallel, other than the use of the word "future." One makes a promise and the other plays to insecurity. The farther down the economic ladder one descends, the more effective the provocative question becomes.

A look toward the future is a compelling sales argument. Every one of these people can be considered pre-retirement, and every one can be assumed to have greater buying power (or to think greater buying power exists) than non-working seniors have.

Of all the categories, this one is the best to select for products and services that can be tied to the working environment —

(Fig. 3–5) This ad is aimed squarely at the "comfortables." Those below this level will have too few dollars to invest; those above it will seek a more sophisticated type of investment.

computer-related items, including user-friendly software; online services and Internet access; car and equipment leasing; and similar items.

Affluent

List brokers charge the most — as they should — for names of affluent seniors. Affluence and "still working" often are the same person, but the appeal differs.

Marketers have a choice of appeals: conferred status or implied status. Conferred status often takes a congratulatory tone; implied status may be better implemented by seeming to take affluence for granted.

More than any other age group other than the occasional lottery-winning nouveau-riche, seniors like to display their affluence. Catering to this has sold many items that otherwise would languish on store shelves — collectibles, dinnerware, automobiles, designer garments.

Cruise lines proselytize heavily within this group. Taking a cruise, to those born before World War II, has always been a sign of affluence. For that matter, many in the "comfortable" category can be upsold to a better grade of cabin by a sales appeal suggesting that cabin position is a reflection of financial substance. Smart telemarketers use this tactic. (If you decide to use the "reflection of financial substance" telemarketing upgrade, use it only on those who already have made a primary commitment to buy, donate, or participate. Using the technique for original sale can scare off those who might have been willing to buy, donate, or participate on a more basic level.)

This group also is grist for the selling-mill of those who market prepaid funerals and burial lots. To some individuals, having made such arrangements is a status symbol.

The Value of *Rapport*

Establishing rapport with any of these groups puts a marketer ahead in the race for the dollar.

In the absence of "beloved" spokespeople and the constant exposure of "scam" deals, rapport is harder and harder to establish. Some marketers shoot themselves in the foot instead of shooting marketing bullets at their targets.

One single word can damage rapport. Single words can cause a senior to rebel against change. One of those words: "Learn."

The word "Learn" can damage response . . . because "Learn" means having to make a major change under pressure. "Learn" is conditional. A schoolchild knows that's why he or she goes to school. A senior is willing to discover but not to learn. Learning suggests moving into new areas *in which others already are comfortable.* So the senior is automatically behind the rest of the pack. Worse than that: It suggests the possibility of failure.

"Learn to speak Spanish in two weeks" in no way is as effective a headline as "Two weeks from now you'll be speaking Spanish."

If you have to transmit the concept of learning, try substituting "Discover" . . . which puts control where it should be, in the hands of the prospect.

The same little rule applies to a word like "need." Don't tell a senior, "This is what you need." Even a doctor has trouble when projecting this *unless* the senior has asked for advice.

No, it isn't "This is what you need"; it's "This is what you want, isn't it?"

Note that wording. Note the ending, ". . . isn't it?" We employ another psychological trick: Opening a question with a positive statement directs the answer: "This is what you want, isn't it?" is more likely to generate a positive reaction than "Is this what you want?"

The way to generate a positive response is by using positive terms. So, with a single exception, don't deal in negatives. Use words with a positive connotation. Avoid words with a negative connotation. The one exception is fund raising, which often achieves results from negative information.

Significance of Recognition

Advertising to seniors simply "as seniors" isn't all that bad an idea, if what you're selling has a universal appeal — for example, religious goods or a health-related product. But if you're buying mailing lists, or if your offer demands a specific economic level for profitable response, or if you want a pinpointed test, recognition of the strata available to you can not only save you money; it can be the difference between a profitable promotion and an unprofitable promotion.

Example: Suppose you're selling leather-bound books — classics whose titles are familiar to this age group. Mailing to over-65s may or may not make money. Mailing to comfortable and/or affluent over-65s has a better chance of making money; and aiming your promotional thrust at motivators which have impact on the comfortable/affluent group has the best chance of making money.

Can you over-stroke, over-flatter? Probably not . . . unless your sales argument comes tromping in like an elephant. But always ask: Do I seem sincere? Have I done my best not to pitch and snort, but to establish rapport?

4

Logical Appeals

The marketer whose entire campaign to seniors is based on the notion that "Bargain!" is the one-string fiddle does have a point — not the only point, but a potent one.

"Bargain!" works, as the text of this book plus many tens of thousands of advertisements and mailers verify. Children have no notion what something costs, nor — and from a marketing point of view this is a stronger comparative — do they have the emotional scar tissue generated by fighting for a superior lifestyle.

Which came first, chicken or egg? Seniors, bombarded by advertising that goads them with "You've worked a lifetime and now you deserve better," expect better. They want discounts on Tuesdays, specials at restaurants, discounts on every kind of ticket from airlines to theatres.

Is their expectation the result of all these promotions? Or are all these promotions the result of their expectation?

For the 21st century marketer, the origin is inconsequential. Fact is what matters, and fact says "Bargain!" works.

Need I repeat a venerable point? $99.95 is *light-years* less expensive than $100.00. But explaining the reverse side of this truism might be of value: When mentioning what a price has been discounted *from*, $100.00 is significantly more effective than $99.95.

These mini-exercises in sales psychology usually puzzle both the message-sender and the message-receiver. Both parties know, firmly and directly and with ample experience of having items such as sales tax push a number well above its minor deduction, that the whole concept is artificial. But artificial or not, rejected intellectually or not, dropping below the previous "10" by even five cents does work . . . even if only on a deeply subliminal emotional level. So why not use it?

Restoring Lost Youth

We have another little psychological rule that helps us sell to the mature marketplace. If you market cosmetics or beauty aids or hair dyes or sexual performance enhancers or skin rejuvenators or weight-loss products, remember this rule:

Restoration outsells preservation.

By that I mean you should tell the reader — and back up your statement with photographs — that whatever you are selling restores a previous condition.

With that concept in mind, which headline will pull the most response?

A)   Remember what a flawless complexion this movie star had? At age 60, she still has a flawless complexion.
B)   Remember what a flawless complexion this movie star had? At age 60, she has a flawless complexion once again.

"B" is a far more powerful claim than "A" because "B" takes full credit for the circumstance. If an aging movie star still has the same flawless complexion she had in her youth, the relationship with what the vendor is selling is weakened.

Nor is prevention of deterioration as salesworthy as the restoration of lost beauty or memory or sexual prowess or bladder control or physical endurance or any of the other prices one pays for aging. Reason: If deterioration is already noticeable, prevention of *further* deterioration is nowhere near as strong a reason to buy as climbing back to a pre-deteriorated condition. (More on this in the next section.)

So unless you can make a medical claim, or at least a pseudo-medical claim, don't say a product will prevent deterioration. That claim does *not* pull as well as saying your preparation will restore a condition from a more youthful time.

This is another one of those complicated points, so elaboration is in order. The statement was, "Unless you can make a medical claim." So for weight loss you wouldn't say what you sell prevents fatness and overweight. You would say what you sell restores the trim body the individual used to enjoy.

For a product that does have medical overtones, we can suggest that what we sell prevents deterioration. This might apply to a compound designed as a prostate medication (Fig. 4–1) or a compound linked to the fear of losing memory (Fig. 4–2). Older folks

(Fig. 4–1) Although "mice-type" — type smaller than 9-point — is usually frowned on when advertising to seniors, this little ad uses it beneficially. It's almost as though the tiny type size is part of the whispered medical advice.

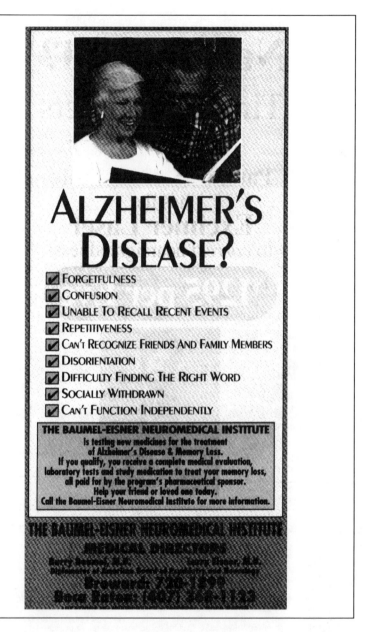

(Fig. 4–2) The key line in this ad: "Help your friend or loved one today."
The ad seems to be mildly deceptive, because the implication is that
treatment is free. Actually, only the evaluation, tests, and "study medication," whatever that is, are free.

resent being told they already have lost some of their memory: "I have not. I'm as sharp as I ever was, Mr. — uh — what's your name again?" But they welcome something that says to them, "Your brain power will remain intact."

The success of latter-day products such as Ginkgo Biloba and Melatonin attest to this facet of marketing.

Health Improvement and Sexual Performance

The natural diminution of sexual prowess among men . . . and mild libidinal decrease among women, especially those who have had a hysterectomy — has led to the establishment of a huge industry.

Parade Magazine commissioned a 1996 study of the sex lives of the over-65s. No surprises:

Seniors who are sexually active — and only about two of five over-65s are — have sex 2.5 times per month. Those surveyed said they'd prefer twice that number.

Medications and weakening of the equipment cause impotence and frustration. They also have spawned a growing industry, ranging from over-the-counter supplements such as ginseng, yohimbe, and muira puama to more dramatic measures such as penile implants and injections which require visits to specialized clinics.

The way to sell sexual satisfaction to seniors doesn't parallel the technique of selling it to younger generations. The problem, usually, is less embarrassing because it is so common within this age group. Therefore, the promise has to be straightforward and unsubtle.

Helpful is the suggestion that sexual dysfunction isn't necessarily related to aging. Fig. 4–3 includes quotes from the total cross-section of age groups — age 26, age 41, age 54, and age 62. (Better: include a 70+ testimonial.)

The testimonials serve another purpose: They become *surrogates* for the target individual, adding a valuable confidence factor.

(Fig. 4–3) This ad, promising help for sexual dysfunction, includes typical "quotes" from a broad range of age-sectors. Seniors will feel less diffident about visiting the center when they see representation, at least in the advertising, by younger age groups.

This technique also applies to hair transplants, plastic surgery, and other age/potency combatants. Subtlety is a weaker sales tool than explicit statements of benefit, because subtlety can't make the promise of regeneration or restoration the individual is looking for.

(Fig. 4–4) The promise of restoration of potency finds a huge acceptance among older men, who view with alarm their flagging powers. Note the absolute promise this ad makes.

An absolute, inviolable rule

We've explored some of the marketing byways for health improvement. But we haven't emphasized the overriding, absolute, inviolable rule of health-product advertising. In two words:

Don't lie.

Don't label this overriding, absolute, inviolable rule a truism until you yourself have skirted close to the edge by overselling or making a questionable claim. The urge to take that one additional step can be overwhelming, especially when competitors are making outrageous claims.

This is where the professional marketer shows his mettle. The professional doesn't write . . .

Does it work? We guarantee it will work.

Rather, the professional writes . . .

Does it work? Only you can tell. But we're your partner in this, and you can't lose . . . because if it doesn't, just tell us so and we'll quickly refund every cent you paid for it.

In this example, the second copy-block is substantially longer than the first. It's no surprise, because a flat statement *should be* shorter than an equivocal statement. We pay a penalty in being unable to make a quick, hard, flat statement. We reap a benefit in better avoidance of unpleasant visits by investigators from the Food & Drug Administration, the Federal Trade Commission, and other nasty government bureaucrats who for some insane reason object to advertising that lies.

A parenthetical point that can save you money:
Notice the last two words of the description we just explored: ". . . *for it.*" Those words were carefully chosen. If you decide that too many seniors are sharpshooting, ordering and using and then returning just as a matter of pure cussedness, your refund won't include the cost of shipping.

Suppose the price is "$49.95 + $3.95 shipping." Those two words, "for it," mean you'll refund the $49.95 but not the $3.95. Make no mistake: This little exception can reduce the number of returns.

Make no second mistake: I'm not recommending you do this; I'm just pointing out the availability of a technique. If you do trust your customers and would-be customers, reverse this exception:

. . . because if it doesn't, just tell us so and we'll quickly refund every cent you paid for it, even including shipping.

Some marketers, reacting to what seems to be chronic blindness among customers who make out a check for the exact amount, *not* including shipping, don't use "$3.95 shipping"; they use "$3.95 shipping/insurance," which seems more profound. "Shipping and handling" bothers many non-seniors as well as seniors, because the idea of having their merchandise "handled" is unappealing.

A philosophy that seems to have considerable merit: Offer a guarantee that *includes* shipping to existing customers and be more careful when wording a guarantee aimed at new buyers. Loyalty — a lost trait among the under-50s — still exists among seniors, who find great comfort in dealing with companies from whom they've had fair treatment before.

Status

A dichotomy exists: Some seniors regard the very fact of having reached age 55, 60, 65, or 70 as the basis for status; others feel defeated.

Both circumstances are grist for the aggressive marketer's word-mill.

For conferring or recognizing status:

Phrases such as "You've earned this" or "You deserve this" or "You've worked hard for this" have a double impact. First, they acknowledge the status; second, they tie whatever the marketer is selling to that status, so the relationship becomes an automatic touchstone.

For counteracting the thought — however subliminal it might be — that age is a step downward:

Phrases such as "The best is yet to come" or "Aren't you glad?" or "Not just moving on . . . moving up" quietly counteract any defeatist attitudes while tying hope for the future to whatever the marketer is selling.

For a marketer uncertain which position his or her advertising should assume, conferring or recognizing status unquestionably is the most promising approach, not only because of two rules of salesmanship — 1) *Positives outpull negatives;* 2) *recognition and conferring of status outpulls suggestion of deficiency* — but also because that magical word, **rapport,** overcomes the skepticism implicit in so many seniors' lack of receptivity to marketing messages.

Figs. 4–5a and 4–5b are two panels from a mailing by a bank to a prospective senior customer. Lists for such mailings usually originate in credit bureaus, so the individual who receives this does indeed have status . . . although the source isn't mentioned in the mailing.

(Figs. 4–5a and 4–5b) This bank uses the smart word *partnership* to describe the anticipated relationship and special benefits for seniors.

A Risky Fund-Raising Weapon: Anger

Professional fund raisers sometimes carry a live grenade in their hands: anger.

It's a live grenade because unless thrown with absolute accuracy, it can go off in your face.

Anger works under only two fund-raising circumstances:

1. An extremist group communicating with members of that group.
2. An exponent of a highly politicized viewpoint circulating a demand for action among those most likely to share the viewpoint.

Examples of no. 2 — environmentalists, ethnic or racial activists, pro- or anti-immigration forces, religious groups reacting to damaging news.

Grandparenting: A Huge Niche Opportunity

Let's not overlook a huge additional marketplace senior citizens open for us. Many of them are grandparents . . . and more and more, as lists become more sophisticated and give us more information about individuals, we can target them as grandparents.

Fig. 4–6 does just that: "Send Your Grandchildren A Gift They'll Love. You." Can you see the psychology behind this ad? It says to the grandparent: "Your grandchildren miss you." The ad builds guilt by suggesting the grandparent *can* visit the grandchildren.

Fig. 4–7 uses grandparenting as a reason to sell portraits of children, bypassing the parent in favor of the grandparents who undoubtedly don't see their grandchildren every day or even every month. Fig. 4–8, the cover of a newspaper insert, is for a toy company; but note the line across the bottom: "10% SENIOR CITIZEN DISCOUNT Every Tuesday."

As an international average, half the population of the world between age 45 and age 59 are grandparents. More than 80 percent of those age 60 or older are grandparents. Some countries are establishing a "Grandparents' Day" — and the entire purpose of

Send Your Grandchildren
A Gift They'll Love. You.

They miss you. So let USAir take you to them for less. If you're 62 or older, you'll save 10% off most flights with our Senior Saver Fare. Plus our Golden Opportunities™ Coupon Books can stretch your dollars even further. Books of four

USAir
USAir begins with you

coupons are available for $596. Eight are only $1,032. So you can fly within the U.S., Canada, and the Islands for as little as $129 one-way. Contact your travel consultant or call USAir at **1(800)428-4322.** Because you're a gift they'll treasure forever.

Prices are subject to change without notice.

(Fig. 4–6) Bright wording and a winsome illustration make this ad a winner. Had the heading been "Now you can see your grandchildren as often as you like," the appeal would have been fractional.

"Grandparents' Day" is to give marketers another reason to sell. So until Grandparents' Day exists, tie sales promotions to Mother's Day and Father's Day.

(Fig. 4–7) Approaching grandparents to buy portraits of their grandchildren is logical marketing. Those familiar with portrait studios will agree that pricing down the first portrait is standard; markups come from additional prints.

Just the tip of the commercial iceberg

But that's just the tip of a commercial iceberg. If you can identify grandparents, you can sell them toys and infant furniture and telephone calls and greeting cards and sporting equipment and travel and subscriptions and education and insurance and investments and cameras, *based on their being grandparents.* You have two big advantages:

First, grandparents usually have more discretionary money to spend than parents do.

Second, grandparents usually have no children living at home. This gives you a *huge* advantage if you know how to put together an emotional sales appeal.

Some marketers target new parents. They pepper them with mail and samples. They give them samples of baby food and sample copies of publications. They telephone them and even make per-

(Fig. 4–8) Grandparents account for a huge percentage of toys, especially in the off-Christmas seasons. The 10% senior citizen discount, common among department stores and health food stores, may seem out of place in a toy store. It isn't.

sonal calls. But they overlook the generation behind those parents . . . a generation able to buy, to give gifts, to enjoy the new baby without having to change diapers. Incidentally, grandparents often give a year's diaper service as a birth gift.

Fig. 4–10 illustrates another kind of gift — life insurance. Few parents think of life insurance for children; but grandparents, whose own sense of mortality is actually in sync with the appearance of grandchildren, are more likely to consider such a "gift."

If you've been mailing promotions to new parents, a suggestion: Include an extra envelope. On that envelope is the legend,

(Fig. 4–9) Using a celebrity in an ad is no novelty. Using a celebrity as a grandparent is. This one will strike home to many who see it.

"For the New Grandparent." Inside the envelope is an offer or a group of offers, with special discounts until the baby is six months old.

(Fig. 4–10) This is the face of a card in a "marriage mailing" (chapter 7 discusses this term). The reverse side of the card calls for a $1 premium to cover the first six months of a $5,000 policy, then $20 a year until the child reaches age 26.

Once you've captured a grandparent's name, you have pure gold. You can continue to extend special offers tied to the child's birthday or education.

The grandparent market is one marketers should milk, because the money is there and the emotional tie is there. If worded right, another benefit is there — the willingness to let *you* worry about what to buy instead of their having to go to a store and wonder if they bought the right item for a child's age group.

The Common Denominator

Although key words such as *bargain* and *restoration* and *happiness* have a can't-miss aura, don't let your marketing run on tracks.

Whenever possible, *test.* That's because your competitors, reading this or figuring out the approach on their own, can use the same motivators you do. Testing keeps you a step ahead.

5

Logical and Illogical Fears, and What to Do About Them

Most children trust everybody.

Most seniors don't trust anybody.

Both those statements are grotesquely overstated generalizations; but both are useful in marketing.

(In fact, the implicit trusting nature of children is the reason for such stringent regulation of advertising aimed at pre-schoolers. Prior to putting these regulations in place, overstatements and trick photography abused juvenile trust.)

Over a span of years, naiveté gives way to skepticism. Digestion of horror stories — "Retiree Bilked of Life Savings" — is the catalyst turning accrued caution into fear of being swindled.

Lawyers pepper seniors with "You've been ripped off" advertising, because seniors are the most likely to believe this has happened. Fig. 5–1 typifies such advertising.

But fear of being defrauded, a venerable qualm, is by no means the only fear seniors hold as a protective shield against the world of commerce. Here are some others:

(Fig. 5–1) This ad, in a publication distributed primarily to seniors, is cleverly constructed. Note the second question which, if answered yes, really suggests the broker did a good job. "They're out to get you!" is heady stuff for seniors.

Fear of Traveling

Traveling poses several fears for seniors — emotional and economic.

Emotional fear stems from the gradual unwillingness to experiment, a common but not universal accompaniment to advancing age. The ancient joke, "I said it to Orville and I said it to Wilbur: The damned thing never will get off the ground!" still has some validity among older folks.

Some, in fact, won't fly if they can't get a seat in the rear of the plane, having convinced themselves that when (not "if") the plane crashes, those in the rear have a greater chance of survival.

Oddly, travel fear doesn't extend to two other areas — cruises and trains. (It often does extend to automobiles. Fig. 5–2 presents an image of Volvo that has cost the car company sales in non-senior groups, so much so that Volvo has a separate "younger image" campaign.) Vacation cruises are loaded with seniors; in fact, they often dominate the passenger list. One reason is the overtone of affluence (see chapter 3) the very word "cruise" suggests to so many seniors; another is the high percentage of retirees, for whom greater availability of leisure time makes possible the concept of leisurely travel.

Some wags say that older drivers have a fear-attachment, all right — the fear of younger drivers that they'll be hit by a wandering senior-driven car. Folklore feeds this anecdote, punctuated by newspaper photographs of seniors who have driven through a plate-glass window or turned right from a left-hand lane. Actually, seniors cause fewer accidents than young beginning drivers, but every year, legislators in one state or another introduce a bill intended to limit the driving privileges of seniors by requiring more frequent examinations for both proficiency and eyesight.

Reacting to this perception, seniors are willing to accept protective options on their insurance coverage. Fear of being involved in an accident or being sued is a genuine fear . . . and a genuine fear is a genuine reason for dynamic advertising whose end product is the soothing of that fear.

Fear of flying . . . and the cost of flying

Senior citizen discounts for multiple trips have been potent sales weapons for airlines. Even though many of these discounts have huge blackout periods and multiple restrictions, the image of a senior citizen lifting the phone at 12:01 a.m., to grab a seat on a flight whose availabilities clear 30 days ahead, is too common to ignore.

Peace of mind included.

Think it over

The Volvo 960

The six-cylinder charisma, the smooth automatic transmission, wheel suspension that straightens out the curves and first-class comfort — they are already enough to make the Volvo 960 a very special car.

As one of the safest cars in the world, it also provides peace of mind — to make your journey all the more uplifting.

The Volvo 960 Series includes estates and saloons, all generously equipped with the very latest in automotive technology. Whichever version you choose, you can combine it with a wide range of options — and have a Volvo 960 to match your very own way of life.

VOLVO

Advanced six-cylinder, 24-valve engine, 2.5- and 3.0-litre versions. Intelligent automatic gearbox. Sophisticated rear suspension. Volvo's complete safety design, including the Side Impact Protection System. Specifications may vary from market to market.

(Fig. 5–2) Volvo in this ad doesn't advertise transportation or comfort or style; it advertises safety. For many seniors, this is the crucial factor when buying a car. (Others let loose and buy their first convertible.)

Of all age and demographic groups, seniors are the most aware of discounts and frequent flyer options. The typical business traveler and probably the majority of vacationers have stringent and

specific time-frames within which travel must be started and completed. Retirees, and also many of the "still working" seniors, have
fewer restrictions. They can travel when the price is best.

No evidence exists that a higher percentage of seniors have a
physical fear of flying, beyond the total universe of passengers.
Most "sweaty palm" classes have few seniors.

A common complaint among first class passengers is "those
people" coming from the nether regions of the plane to use the first
class washroom. Airlines can capitalize on this, if they like, by en-
hancing the "Travel economy . . . feel first class" aspect of their
flights. Evidence of the senior invasion into the first class cabin may
be anecdotal, but if true, it's unsurprising: Numerous members of
this age group are taking advantage of what they believe they've
earned — the right to demand as much as appears to be available.

Technological Fears

Historically, change came slowly. Seniors probably weren't
among the first to adopt the wheel in place of a wooden sledge,
because the average life span was about 30. But seniors did exist
when the typewriter was invented, and they *weren't* among the first
to use that newfangled gadget.

This isn't because seniors resist innovation; rather, it's because
the comfort level with the familiar increases as aging brings occasional (or frequent) disappointments when one departs from the
familiar. Some of the more common manifestations are resistance
to changes in fashion . . . demand in supermarkets for brands no
longer carried . . . irritation when daily routine is interrupted . . .
and in a large number of cases, keeping a television set tuned to a
single station, regardless of what programs are being shown.

(One reason cruises are popular among seniors is the slow-to-
change nature of this recreation.)

Technologically, seniors have been among the last to comput-
erize on a personal level, to join an online service, and to dip a toe
in the Internet. Few writers in their 20s, 30s, 40s, and even 50s still
create their texts in longhand on a yellow pad; many seniors do.

Announcing a special deal for AARP members.
Computer, printer and software only $1,899.

While supplies last, you can purchase an Apple® Macintosh® Performa® 5215 with an Apple StyleWriter® 1200 for only $1,899, plus shipping and sales tax. Included is a full range of software, like ClarisWorks for writing letters and Quicken for managing your money. You'll also get full Internet access with eWorld, an easy way to communicate with friends and grandchildren (most of whom are using a Mac® in school). We've even added some special extras, like Willmaker, to help you make plans for the future. Route 66, to map out your trips. And Ultimate Solitaire, to hone your playing skills. For complete information and financing details, just call **800-780-5011.**

Available only to AARP members. CPU includes 75 MHz PowerPC 603 microprocessor, 8MB RAM, 1GB hard drive. Only one purchase per member. Good only while supplies last. ©1996 Apple Computer, Inc. All rights reserved. Apple, the Apple logo, Macintosh, Performa and StyleWriter are registered trademarks of Apple Computer, Inc. Mac is a trademark of Apple Computer, Inc. All Macintosh computers are designed to be accessible to individuals with disability. To learn more (US only), call 800-795-7585 or TTY 800-755-0601.

Fig. 5–3 offers a computer "deal" to seniors. The text is tailored precisely to appeal to every logical member of this age group.

Sometimes resistance to change is based on a strong feeling that "I've learned enough in my lifetime, and it's unfair to keep hounding me to learn even more about subjects and equipment I never was interested in before." Sometimes the resistance is based on economics. And sometimes the resistance is based on a genuine fear of change.

Yet, because peer-group awareness equals that of the 12-to-18

(Fig. 5–3) This computer ad, in a publication distributed exclusively to seniors, combines "a special deal" with reassurance that this will be "an easy way to communicate with friends and grandchildren (most of whom are using a Mac™ in school)."

group, once a brave pioneer breaks the barrier, others become willing to pile into the breach. This is why, in a computer store, older people seek out older salespeople.

Ah! Here we have a non-secret, tied to all the other principles in this book. Oldsters can sell oldsters where youngsters can't. This is true not only of computers but of fashions, cosmetics, and automobiles.

Of course it's a non-secret! The parallel is doing business with a co-religionist. The comfort level is high, and rapport is half-accomplished as the potential transaction begins.

Step by step is the way to go

Impatience doesn't pay off when marketing to seniors. One reason infomercials are effective when aimed at this group is that the format is both more leisurely and more step-by-step. If selling and information are integrated and handled properly, the individual feels he or she is making the decision gradually, without coercion.

Seniors have fewer compunctions about admitting they're unable to operate a piece of equipment than are other demographic groups. So classes and seminars are much in order. Adding refreshments to the classes often brings attendance from those who otherwise wouldn't attend; but careful, please: Any retailer who has held an "Open House" has horror stories to tell about shameless seniors who stuff purses and pockets with hors d'oeuvres. The decision has to be between wanting more people present or using the class-cum-refreshment as a post-sale event.

(This becomes a philosophical decision. Time-share sales organizations want bodies on hand; computer retailers want cash in hand before largesse.)

Step-by-step hands-on, carefully prepared to yield optimum results, will also yield sales to those who come into a store or office claiming they'll never be able to operate the equipment. Only partially does this parallel a test drive when demonstrating an automobile; these people know how to drive and have, in fact, been behind the wheel long before the salesperson was born.

A logical suggestion for marketing to seniors anything requiring an operational knowledge: Keep it simple. The words "user-friendly" are suspect, because many within this group have electronic gear — even clocks — sitting idle and unused. The VCRs flash at 12:00. Whether this is because of inability to operate these items or unwillingness to penetrate even a simple instruction manual is *of no consequence*. What matters is transforming the individual into a customer.

The advantage is that rarest of customer traits, *loyalty*. Once a senior becomes convinced that you're the source — the kindly, understanding, nonjudgmental source — even a major gaffe might not rip the relationship. That's a key advantage of having a senior as a customer or client: The individual will defend not only his/her choice of you but your business practices as well.

Insurance Fears

It's certainly no secret, even among those affected by it, that many seniors not only have no idea what their insurance coverage is; they may have two or three policies covering the identical potential troubles . . . even extending to multiple coverage of Medicare Part "B."

Is this good or bad?

It depends who you are. If you're an unscrupulous insurance salesperson, it's good, because you can sell insurance based on *fear* — fear of being unable to pay for necessary prescriptions or a necessary operation; fear of being forced to recover at home instead of in an attended nursing facility; fear of being regarded as a charity patient; fear of dying and being buried in a potter's field.

These are potent fears, and those who cater to them by naked appeals to those fears often succeed far beyond any realistic expectations. Advertising with a "What if you . . ." approach demands — and gets — intensive readership.

Fig. 5–4 is pure "fear" — "Medicare alone won't cover. . . ." The illustration strikes home to many seniors who visualize themselves in that same painful circumstance.

(Fig. 5–4) Fear of being underinsured and not covered for emergencies drives many to supplement their coverage. This ad ends with a lightning strike: "You can take your chances with Medicare alone, you can pay for the extra coverage, or you can save your money with PCA QualiCare."

Understand, please: An appeal to fear doesn't mean the advertiser is a charlatan. The charlatan just uses this easy-to-grab handle.

Allaying insurance fears also can be achieved by the arm-around-the-shoulder technique . . . the friendly advisor.

Fig. 5–5 gives us more clues if we are selling insurance to seniors. The heading of this ad is, "A lot of members think it's too complicated to choose the right supplemental health insurance. So we made it easy."

A lot of members think it's too complicated to choose the right supplemental health insurance.

So we made it easy.

Just call our toll-free number. You'll talk with a friendly, experienced Prudential customer service representative who'll be happy to answer your questions. Your representative will also send you an easy-to-understand Free Information Kit you can review at your leisure. So, finding the coverage you need – and the benefits you want – is easy.

Find out more about the supplemental health insurance plans offered by the AARP Group Health Insurance Program, provided by The Prudential Insurance Company of America. Call toll-free or return the coupon today for your Free Information Kit, including the facts on benefits, costs, eligibility, limitations, and exclusions. Of course, there's no obligation.

1-800-245-1212, Operator #92
Monday - Friday, 9 a.m. - 8 p.m.

≈ AARP Group Health Insurance Program

Prudential

The Prudential Insurance Company of America (licensed in all states) Fort Washington, PA 19034. Not connected with or endorsed by the U.S. Government or the Federal Medicare Program. All plans may not be available in your state. Group Policy Nos. G-36000-2-4-10. AARP's Medicare Supplement Plans do not duplicate Medicare's benefits, and unless specifically stated, will only pay for benefits that are Medicare eligible expenses. All plans may not be available in all states in persons eligible for Medicare by reason of disability. Long Term Care plans are not available in Delaware, Kansas, Maryland, Minnesota, New Hampshire or Wisconsin and are available only to AARP members age 50-79 who meet certain eligibility requirements.

Please send my Free Information Kit.   [280]

1) I'd like to know more about AARP's: 3) My date of birth is:
   ☐ Medicare Supplement   ___/___/___
      Insurance Plans   Month Day Year
   ☐ Group Hospital Insurance Plans   4) Name _____
   ☐ Long Term Care   (Mr., Ms., Mrs., Miss) Please print.
      Insurance Plans   Address _____
                    City _____
2) My AARP membership number is: State ____ Zip _____
                    Phone # _____
   (See your mailing label for number.)   (Area Code)

Mail to: AARP Group Health Insurance Program, P.O. Box 25601, Lehigh Valley, PA 18002-5601
The Prudential Insurance Company of America

(Fig. 5–5) "So we made it easy" builds confidence, seems to eliminate any "small print" obfuscation, and has the tone of utter friendliness.

The insurance company tries to position itself as friendly advisor. As we'll see in subsequent chapters, the psychology is sound, and those able to implement it can mine golden age gold.

Seniors may regard the message of fig. 5–6 as even friendlier: "Start a $10,000 life insurance policy for $1." That's the way to get them to send in the coupon. And notice the photograph: It's the standard senior citizen advertising photo, a healthy-looking older couple.

Fig. 5–7 is a letter that begins with what we call a "Johnson Box" — a message above the greeting. Notice how the first sentence absolutely targets seniors: "Here's great news if you're between the ages of 50 and 75." Obviously, the list has been chosen to include only those between the ages of 50 and 75, although the slant is heavily toward the higher end.

(Fig. 5–6) Analyze the photograph in this ad: What's the purpose of the basket of flowers? If your guess is that it helps the lyrical, pleasant, non-threatening tone of the message, then your guess is the same as mine. Mail-order life insurance to seniors has to emphasize two points: 1) It's guaranteed renewable; 2) No physical exam. This ad does both.

Some marketers know how to capitalize on fear. Fig. 5–8a is the front cover of a catalog called "Mature Wisdom" — a complete catalog dedicated to products for older people.

Mutual of Omaha Companies

```
* * * * * * * * * * * * * * * * * * * * * * * * * * * *
*   Here's great news if you're between the ages of  *
*   50 and 75!  You can choose from four plans,      *
*   providing as much as $10,000 life insurance --   *
*   for a very affordable cost.  And you can't be     *
*   turned down for this life insurance ... even      *
*   if you're in poor health.  You are guaranteed     *
*   this insurance.                                    *
* * * * * * * * * * * * * * * * * * * * * * * * * * * *
```

Dear Friend,

What I said above really <u>is</u> good news! It's so good that I urge you to send in your application and payment today!

I'm talking about our EASY WAY life insurance policy. It has so many great features I'll have trouble describing them all in this letter. So I better start right now. Here's a brief listing of advantages this policy brings you:

✔ You buy it by mail -- with no medical exam and no questions to answer about your health.

✔ It insures you for your entire life. (At age 100, you receive the full policy amount.) You can't be canceled because of age or poor health.

✔ You never get a rate increase either because of age or health. And the amount of your insurance is never reduced because of health or age.

✔ You can't be turned down for EASY WAY for <u>any</u> reason -- as long as you're between 50 and 75. Even if you have cancer or heart trouble -- even if you have a dangerous occupation or hobby. We guarantee to accept your application.

✔ Pays benefits for death due to illness or injury. In order to guarantee your acceptance, death benefits payable for natural causes are reduced during the first two years you own the plan -- 125% of the annual premium in the first year, and 250% in the second year. After

over, please

United of Omaha Life Insurance Company · MUTUAL OF OMAHA PLAZA · OMAHA, NE 68175 · 800-733-3114

(Fig. 5–7) The "Johnson Box" says the recipient "can't be turned down, even if you're in poor health." Note how the checkmarks seem to answer every possible objection or question the reader might conceivably have. Reassurance such as this will bring response from seniors.

(Fig. 5–8a) This is the cover of a catalog whose very title makes it clear the contents are aimed at seniors. The model seems to be in her late 30s or early 40s . . . or is it 50s? The image is one of smart contemporaneousness, and the low price of the cover item invites the recipient to open the catalog.

Fig. 5–8b is an item the catalog offers for sale. The heading says, "You're never alone with Safe-T-Man." The beginning of the description of this item: "Designed for use as a visual deterrent,

You're never alone with Safe-T-Man

F. Designed for use as a visual deterrent, Safe-T-Man tricks others into thinking you have the protection of a male companion. Made to appear 6', 175-lbs., he weighs only 4-lbs., easy to move and transport. Sit him in your car, or even by a window when you leave home. Safe-T-Man has latex hands and a soft fabric body. Can be dressed to your liking (clothing not included). USA.
A777029, Safe-T-Man, $99.95 or 4 interest-free payments of $25.00
A776682, Button on legs, **$19.95**

INTEREST-FREE **4** PAYMENTS

of 25.00 on Visa or MasterCard

(Fig. 5–8b) In the pages of the catalog whose cover is fig. 5–8a is this item — "Safe-T-Man." The inset drawings show the versatility of this doll/ puppet in various positions and with various costumes. Older women, seeing this item and relating "the protection of a male companion" to any real or imagined fright episodes, will respond.

Safe-T-Man tricks others into thinking you have the protection of a male companion." Aimed at women of any age — in fact, occasionally the newspapers carry the story of younger women using this to appear to have two persons in the car when driving in a high-occupancy-vehicle lane on the expressway — it becomes especially effective when seen by older women, whose visions of late-night attacks are too often real.

(Fig. 5–9) "Your loved ones could get nothing!" Every senior has heard of such circumstances. Selling a "will kit" as a kit would bring no response; selling it as "What happens if you die . . . and leave no will?" caters to a well-justified fear.

Shopping Fears

Seniors have three distinct sets of shopping fears: 1) retail shopping; 2) service companies; 3) shopping by mail.

These are neither identical nor even parallel, except as they relate to the general fear of being defrauded. The fear sometimes is so apparent that retail clerks trample one another getting out of the way so they won't face the multiplicity of questions that may well, if not answered exactly as predetermined, result in an hour or more of wasted time, sale not completed. Service companies selling home improvements may make a sales call and never return, based on a sour history of dealing with seniors. Mail-order companies steel themselves against correspondence from consumer protection agencies.

These are, admittedly, extreme cases; but such cases are infinitely more common when dealing with seniors than with the general public.

If all is so negative, why bother with seniors at all?

That's an easy one: They have buying power, they aren't universally embittered, and once seniors become your customers (as mentioned before in this chapter) they're fiercely loyal.

Retail fears and what to do about them

Retailers can reduce fear by a number of logical marketing steps. The first three also apply to other types of businesses:

- Emphasize the company's longevity.
- Emphasize the length of time one or more of the principals has been in business.
- If neither of the first two applies, total the number of years of business experience of all principals and advertise it just that way — "You're dealing with a total of 35 years in this business."
- Offer a discount on a specific business day (traditionally, Tuesday) to seniors only.
- Establish a "Club" with Privileged Member Cards.

- Use peer-group salesmanship — older clerks and salespeople to wait on older customers, who invariably have greater confidence in their apparent peers.
- Avoid raucous background music in the store — although this can be a misstep if Generation-X is your major target group and seniors are a minor ancillary.
- If a large store, have an elderly "greeter" on hand.

Service company fears and what to do about them

The first three parallel retailer techniques:

- Emphasize the company's longevity.
- Emphasize the length of time one or more of the principals has been in business.
- If neither of the first two applies, total the number of years of business experience of all principals and advertise it just that way — "You're dealing with a total of 35 years in this business."
- Emphasize an absolute guarantee.
- Include discount coupons in space advertising, with an expiration date. This will bring business from those who ignore conventional service advertising.
- Carry a large tablet and handwrite specifics on it while the prospective senior customer watches. This is far more effective than pre-printed information because it's far more personal and apparently specific-related.
- Emphasize bargain. Create a bargain and then lower it.
- Reassure constantly during installation or work activity, pointing out advantages and asking repeatedly for buyer confirmation of those advantages.
- As the work is being done, give the buyer some sort of gift in exchange for the names of friends who might be interested in what you sell. This serves two purposes — it solidifies the relationship and helps prevent post-sale carping.

- Avoid initiating post-sale contact. This is sticking your head into the lion's mouth.

Mail order fears and what to do about them

Seniors will respond by mail rather than phone in a higher ratio than any other group. Both mail and phone offer fear-allaying procedures:

- Immediately send a "Welcome!" letter acknowledging phone orders. This cuts down refusals and returns.
- Feature happy older people in your advertising.
- Ship orders fast. Some seniors actually forget they've ordered an item. (This is also true of many non-seniors.)
- Implement an "Examine it at our risk" policy. This may seem to be dangerous but it's effective mail order practice on all levels. ("Our risk" doesn't mean "no payment"; it means a guarantee of a full refund.)
- If you know your prospect, "Send no money now" is heavy ammunition; to cold lists, it can result in heavy (and often fruitless) "pay up" correspondence.
- Include a discount certificate, against the next purchase, with every order you ship. The coupon should have an expiration date.
- If you have to add sales tax, do so prominently. Seniors are infamous for ignoring sales tax when paying for a by-mail order.
- For multibuyers — those who have ordered a second time — send a gift. It needn't be a major gift, but a folding umbrella or a box of greeting cards or an inexpensive digital watch will cement a relationship and pay for itself many times over. Be sure to include a very personal note with the gift.

A parenthetical note:

When you ask for "phone number" in the coupon or order form, put it after the space for "address," not before.

Why? Simple psychology. Most people regard their addresses as information they're expected to give you. So we ask for information they expect to give before we ask for information they don't expect to give.

Conclusion

This is just a scraping of the possible ways to allay fears, both logical and illogical. The smart marketer doesn't sneer at seniors; rather, the smart marketer works within their experiential background. It's hard, in a brutalized society, to live 60 or more years without compiling some horror stories of ill-treatment and outright deceit on the part of vendors. Marketers who want business only from naive buyers should themselves face a fear — fear of prosecution for misrepresentation.

Treating the senior buyer as a partner, with honor, and flavoring the relationship with old-fashioned salesmanship, will bring business. Maximize the offer — but don't lie.

6

Spelling Out Benefit

Let's analyze the way communication techniques of the 1990s have split society into groups who don't share one another's culture (or lack of it), their motivations, their buying power, or even what they accept as symbols of success.

An easy example: automobile advertising. Automobile manufacturers deliberately aim their advertising at specific age groups.

Jeep or Audi aim their advertising at a younger age group than the luxury cars. The typical senior, comfortable behind the wheel of even a vintage Cadillac or Lincoln, is befuddled by the term "4x4" and may think "MacPherson Struts" are dance steps. In fact, four-wheel drive can be a negative, because it suggests roads which are full of mud and holes.

The demographics of ownership of those various brands of automobiles prove that this type of advertising — we call this *vertical* advertising, because it eliminates more people than it includes — results in sales.

What we never can be positive about is whether the advertiser is making a mistake by steering his advertising toward a specific group. And the manufacturers are aware of this. Volvo changes its advertising, emphasizing speed and style, trying to attract the younger buyers. When Audi creates "hot car" advertising it aims that advertising at younger buyers; when it creates advertising stressing safety it aims that advertising at older buyers.

Sometimes a split image is confusing. And confusion damages both image and sales. We have an obvious rule for this:

Buying interest decreases in exact ratio to an increase in confusion.

Avoiding Confusion

How do we avoid confusion? Two ways:

1. We advertise in vertical media. An advertisement in a publication aimed at seniors reaches only seniors. An advertisement aimed at what we call "Generation-X" reaches only people in their 20s. Seniors wouldn't bother to read magazines aimed at Generation-X even if they were the only magazines on the airplane.
2. We use direct mail. Direct mail is the only 100 percent *targeted* medium. (I'm excluding telemarketing and personal sales calls because these aren't really mass media.)

In space advertising aimed at seniors, you can help yourself to avoid confusion by being certain you tell the reader what you're selling, *within five seconds.* Seniors don't have the patience younger buyers have. They draw a quick conclusion: "I understand this," or, "I don't understand this." Promise a benefit early and they'll read your advertising. If you're tricky or subtle, they'll *not* read your advertising.

You can see that selling to seniors requires at least a primitive grasp of sales psychology. One way of implementing that psychology is to sell a preferential benefit — that is, a benefit exclusively for this group of readers — on the grounds that the reader has earned the benefit, or uniquely qualifies for it. You apparently appeal to logic. *Apparently.* What you actually are doing is appealing to an emotional response which says, "Yes, I deserve that." For example, this is how you might apparently appeal to logic:

— You've driven safely all your life.
   Why should you pay the same rate as those who. . . .
— Do you ride a bike or play tennis or golf? Then you deserve the kind of coverage designed for active, vital. . . .

Get to the Point

That quick, hard, pointed, targeted apparent appeal to logic gives us another key to grabbing and holding the attention of seniors:

Get to the point.

Tell them, in what appears to be a straightforward and helpful manner, why you're contacting them. Get to the point. We agree subtlety doesn't work. We agree we should tell them what we are selling, quickly. Get to the point. Marketers lose millions, perhaps billions of dollars because the creative team has no knowledge of how to approach this group or regards them as just part of the total consumer universe. Of course they *are* part of the total consumer universe, but they're a distinct and independent segment. Whether in a piece of advertising or a piece of mail, get to the point.

Get to the point!

Getting to the point is easy, very easy, if you use one of these little tools. You may have thought you were getting to the point because you list a batch of features. But a proper sales approach is not one in which *you* think you've been specific; rather, it's one in which the senior individual says to himself or herself, "Oh, I see."

So here are four automatic ways of getting to the point:

— "For example . . ."
— "Why? Because . . ."

— "The reason is . . ."
— "I have something you want."

When you say, "For example," you *force* yourself to give an example. And when you give an example, you get to the point. One caution, please: Be certain the individual understands your example. If your example to seniors has to do with an MTV star or rollerblading, you might have been better off had you *not* given an example.

When you say, "Why, because . . ." you *force* yourself to explain why. And when you explain why, you get to the point. One caution, please: Be certain your explanation makes sense to the individual, within that individual's own experiential background. Don't explain on a level above the individual's capacity to understand, or, worse, by using an assumption the individual resents. This means studying the senior market and knowing what seniors know.

When you say, "The reason is . . ." you *force* yourself to give a reason. And when you give a reason, you get to the point. One caution, please: Be certain the reason you give makes sense to the individual, within that individual's own experiential background.

When you say, "I have something you want," you *force* yourself to name something. And when you name something, you get to the point. For this one, *two* cautions, please: First, be quick to describe an irresistible benefit. Name the benefit *before* naming whatever you're selling. Then, identify what you're selling as the source of that benefit. Be certain the benefit you describe makes sense to the individual, within that individual's own experiential background.

And even more valuable to us, as primitive but professional psychologists: We have to make the desire appear to be achievable. We have to stimulate our targets to think: "Yes, I not only have decided I want this but I have the capability of buying it and using it and benefiting from it."

Do you know why all these little psychological rules are valid? Do you know why they work, when straight descriptions or a lot of adjectives puffing up your product or service without tying that product or service to your target individual will not work? Do you know why they're true?

They're true because even if your claim of superiority is true, that claim of superiority means nothing to the reader unless it relates to him or her. Truth is fact, but fact alone will not sell for you, not to seniors nor to anyone. Fact is cold, dispassionate, without emotion. Fact is a piece of cloth. If you want to sell a suit, tailor that cloth into a suit. Tailoring your fact transforms a raw fact into a suitable appeal.

The Law of Effective Communications

The Law of Effective Communications comes to our aid when we try to inject that magical word *benefit* into the selling mixture:

No amount of "puffery" or self-applause can sell as effectively as a listing of specific benefits. Puffery sometimes works as a means of selling to the very young. Remember the automatic skepticism of your senior targets, and you won't make that dreadful mistake when advertising to this group.

Fig. 6–1 lists specific benefits, tied directly to age. Fig. 6–2 specifies discounts, tied to AARP membership. The credibility of these ads — discounts aren't named in dollars — stems from stating a *reason* for the discounts.

You can see how simple — and how complicated — selling to seniors can be. You can see how getting to the point gives us a huge competitive advantage over others who don't get to the point.

Really, all this can be condensed into three words: Specifics outsell generalizations. This is another one of those truisms all marketers agree is valid . . . but too often don't remember when creating messages designed to cause the reader, viewer, or listener to perform a specific act as the direct result of having absorbed the message. How can the reader perform a specific act if the marketer fails to specify what that act is supposed to be? How can a marketer expect the reader to react enthusiastically unless that marketer gets to the point?

How to Reach Our Targets

What *is* our point? Do we really know how to reach our targets, even when we single them out and advertise or mail specifically to them?

THE SENIORS' CHOICE DISCOUNT.
IT JUST GETS BETTER WITH AGE.

THE SAVINGS JUST KEEP GETTING BETTER WITH PEARLE'S SENIORS' CHOICE CARD. TO RECEIVE YOUR CARD, BRING THIS AD IN TO ANY PARTICIPATING PEARLE VISION, ALONG WITH PROOF OF AGE. IF YOU'RE 50 OR OVER, RECEIVE AT LEAST 50% OFF THE REGULAR PRICE OF *either* FRAME **OR** LENSES WHEN YOU BUY A COMPLETE PAIR OF PRESCRIPTION GLASSES (FRAME AND LENSES). DISCOUNT APPLIES TO THE LOWER PRICED ITEM. SO COME IN TO PEARLE AND GET THE CARD THAT KEEPS GETTING BETTER WITH TIME.

> **THE SENIORS' CHOICE DISCOUNT**
>
> Save 50% if you're 50-59
>
> Save 60% if you're 60-69
>
> Save 70% if you're 70-79
>
> Save 80% if you're 80-89
>
> Save 90% if you're 90-99
>
> Save 100% if you're 100+

PEARLE VISION™

For The Location Nearest You Call 1-800-YES-EYES

Not valid with EyeBuys® or any other frame and lens combination pricing. No other coupons or discounts apply. Program subject to change without prior notice. Some lens restrictions and prescription exclusions may apply. Valid at participating Pearle locations. Comprehensive eye exams available from an independent Doctor of Optometry next door to Pearle. © 1994 Pearle, Inc.

(Fig. 6–1) "The Seniors' Choice Discount" is absolutely specific, by age range, and it gains immediate credibility by the huge discounts offered to octogenarians and above.

(Fig. 6–2) "Save $15 on Weekly Rates" and "Get a Free Weekend Day" are specific benefits for seniors. The discounts are spelled out in great detail. Here is another example of choosing smaller type to add details. When those details relate to benefit, seniors will read them.

Even today, most conventional advertising agencies will think they reach the senior citizen market when they tell a photographer: "For the seniors, replace young people with older people. They should look healthy and have silver hair, not white. Make them look athletic, because seniors don't want to identify with fat, flabby-looking models."

So the photographer shoots a second set of pictures using older models, and the agency is happy. They equate their approach with the tested exercise machine ads and think they've solved the fragmentation problem, because the ad has older people in it, doesn't it? And that reaches the senior market.

Oh, does it?

They're right in one respect: Seniors are more likely to look at print or broadcast advertising if they can identify with the images. A wife of a man over age 55 might *avoid* buying her husband this men's fragrance — "Safari," by Ralph Lauren (Fig. 6–3) — *because*

(Fig. 6–3) Most seniors have a zero identification factor with this ad, not because the models are young but because of the implied lifestyle.

neither she nor her husband looks like either of the models in this photograph.

On the other hand, she might buy Giorgio Armani for her husband, visualizing him in place of the romantically-positioned model in an ad (Fig. 6–4). Wish-fulfillment is part of the psychol-

(Fig. 6–4) This ad is for a man's fragrance (*eau pour homme)*; both men and women seniors might buy the item, the women for their husbands or late-year "significant others," because nothing about the ad turns either men or women off. The model is clean-cut; the woman is unidentifiable. The concept of romance might flare briefly.

ogy of seniors. That's why products which suggest restoration of lost powers are so effective with this group.

Triggering the Senior Response

Here are what we might call "trigger words" for seniors:

- Discount
- Buy direct
- Have a problem with . . . ?
- Do you remember how *[WHATEVER]* used to be?
- Have you considered?

No one familiar with marketing to seniors has to explain that word "Discount." Seniors firmly believe they've earned the right to get a better price. Restaurants have "Early-Bird" dinner prices aimed at seniors. Many department stores set aside Tuesday or Wednesday as days on which seniors who belong to their "Buyers's Club" can get a 10 percent discount on any purchases.

Fig. 6–5 is the *cover* of a catalog. A smiling couple wear matching T-shirts with the legend, "SENIOR CITIZEN — Gimme My Damn Discount!" Sophisticated seniors chuckle at this, but they chuckle knowingly, recognizing "discount" as a prime trigger word. That this appears on the cover of a catalog shows how accepting the entire world of commerce has become, regarding this attitude.

A favored position

"Buy direct" also suggests a special, favored position. We cater to seniors' belief that this is a benefit they deserve. By telling them they can buy direct, we suggest they can avoid the multiple mark-ups others pay. This is pure exclusivity, and exclusivity is labeled throughout this book as one of the great senior motivators, not only of our time but probably of the 21st century . . . in which people are even more likely than they are now to be regarded as units and numbers, not individuals.

Seniors, after all, remember the pre-zip-code era when phone exchanges were Butterfield-8 and Lakeview-5, not 288 and 525. They remember when a bank teller looked for a signature, not a

(Fig. 6–5) This is the cover illustration of a gift catalog. A generation ago, giving someone a T-shirt with this legend would have been considered outrageous. In today's wide-open society, few seniors would worry about wearing the T-shirt in public, and many undoubtedly bought one not as a gift but as a personal choice.

code number. So exclusivity — the "only you" concept — will un-questionably gain in potency as individuals lose more and more individuality in the world of commerce.

Mature people have had a lifetime to compare their achieve-ments with their friends, their neighbors, their co-workers, and their family members. An appeal based on exclusivity has unusual power with this group, because exclusivity suggests an achievement — and it can be a mild achievement, as mild as owning something the neighbor or friend or co-worker doesn't have — an achievement which can cause envy by others.

So when you can't think of any other approach, this one can be effective in convincing older people to respond:

You have worked hard and deserve this special offer that will not be made to others.

This combines exclusivity with privilege. It says to the reader, "Everybody wants it . . . nobody can get it . . . except you." It says to the reader, "Only you . . . only from us." Combining exclusivity with privilege not only is easy; it's as effective as many of the more complex, more sophisticated sales appeals, and often it's consider-ably better, because it appeals to seniors *as seniors*.

Fig. 6–6 has as its heading: "Best way to enjoy what you've earned." The body copy slips, with "After fifty years of hotel ex-perience, we feel age should have its rewards." To many seniors, age isn't the reward-earner; it's the accumulation of miniature successes that need to be recognized.

Chapter 10 points out that "You've earned it" is so serviceable it one day might burn itself out. Or, like "Free" and "New," it might survive forever.

Fig. 6–7 is another example of combining exclusivity with privilege: "Why wait . . . you can have it all now!" The "Gather ye rosebuds while ye may" concept, written in the 17th century by Robert Herrick in a poem titled "To the Virgins, to Make Much of Time," has a totally different logical target in the 21st century. It appeals to the common feeling among older folks that they'd better start cashing in on the special benefits they've earned.

After fifty years of hotel experience, we feel age should have its rewards. That's why all AARP members receive 10% off regular room rates at any of our 3,400 Best Western locations worldwide. And most hotels also offer mature guests some little extras like complimentary room upgrades, continental breakfasts, free local phone calls and a newspaper. Or perhaps you can take advantage of special late check-outs and sleep in. To make your vacation more memorable, bring the grandchildren along for free at many locations.

MATURE BENEFITS FOR GUESTS OVER 50.

For reservations call your travel agent or Best Western at 1-800-603-2277. Or book your next stay with us via the Internet on TravelWeb at: http://www.bestwestern.com/best.html. Because we treat our guests the best.

BEST WAY TO ENJOY WHAT YOU'VE EARNED.

1-800-603-2277
YOUR BEST BET IS A BEST WESTERN.

©1995 Best Western International, Inc. All Best Western Hotels are independently owned and operated.

(Fig. 6–6) "You've earned it" is a staple among approaches to seniors. This ad offers a 10 percent discount off regular room rates, as the "best way to enjoy what you've earned."

Easy copy-helpers

"Have a problem with . . . ?" tells the reader we can solve the problem. If that problem has to do with changes in social structure or living conditions or investments or planning for the future or politics, chances are seniors are our best targets. We solve their problem. We're their surrogates in a hostile social order. We say to them, "Yes, we know the world is changing for the worse. But we are here to fight against these nasty changes."

"Do you remember how *[something or other]* used to be?" is pure nostalgia. Many seniors yearn for bygone times. That's why companies selling recordings of songs from the 1950s and 1960s aim their messages at seniors. These are the people who are bewildered by rock music and mindless shouting and electric guitars. They're delighted to see that others share their view, and they respond to such offers.

(Fig. 6–7) "Why wait for these benefits?" gains strength in ratio to the reader's recognition of his or her own mortality. This is why it has become such a popular theme in advertising to seniors.

Fig. 6–8 appeared in a magazine distributed to seniors. Nostalgia for these bygone movie epics — some were released in 1938 and one in 1935 — drives the sale.

"Have you considered . . . ?" is on this list because it's a small safeguard against launching into a sales argument too quickly. "Have you considered . . . ?" seems to be rational thinking, not high-pressure salesmanship. Obviously, the effectiveness of "Have you considered . . . ?" depends on the words that follow. They should

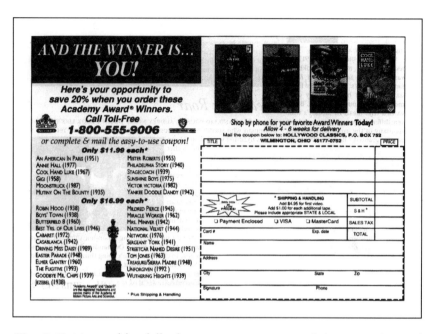

(Fig. 6–8) Many older folks have seen every one of these movies and remember them fondly. An ad in a general-circulation magazine would have to include current releases to pay for itself. Note: This ad says "Allow 4–6 weeks for delivery." However necessary that disclaimer might be, it can be the cause of missed sales, canceled orders, and returns.

suggest the possibility of danger lurking ahead . . . or of a simple, uncomplicated change that will improve the enjoyment of life . . . or of an existing circumstance you, as a friend, remind the reader exists for him or for her and if possible for you as well.

These are by no means the only trigger words for seniors. They're a serviceable starter group. You can build your own list, using these as a base, as you refine your own approaches.

You don't need imagination to use these

The next group of openings works even on days when your imagination has abandoned you. These openings are attention-grabbers when writing a message to seniors:

• *"If you're [WHATEVER], we want to talk to you."* This is another psychological trick. We create a category which fits the reader and then add an "If" clause. We say to the reader, "If you're one of these special people, this is a private message for you." Of course it isn't actually private; but the reader is drawn into our web. This opening works even if all we say is, "If you're over age 55 and want to live to be 95, we want to talk to you"; or, "If you're a successful, mature executive, we want to talk to you."

• *"You asked for this."* We have *two* uses of this opening. The first is when the recipient of our message actually has asked for information. This could be the result of a provocative space or broadcast advertisement which offers details on request. The second is when we make an assumption on behalf of the entire phylum of seniors. We can defend the opening on the ground that senior citizens as a class have asked for whatever we're selling.

"You asked for this" has the benefit of generating *guilt*, one of the great motivators of the late 1990s. Someone who has asked for anything — *anything*, whether it might be information or an actual product, feels guilty if he or she rejects whatever he or she has actually requested.

• *"As seen on TV."* That an item has appeared on television — even in a mail-order commercial — adds cachet to its image. Having been on television is itself a credential to many seniors. Usually (fig. 6–9) "As seen on TV" appears in a TV-screen-shaped box.

Fig. 6–10 goes one step beyond, using "As seen on TV" as a touchstone: "Priced much lower than one seen on TV!"

• *"Special Bonus Offer expires in 7 days."* The hook is obvious — an expiration date; and an expiration date improves response. "Special Bonus Offer" bestows a rationale to the expiration date: Whatever we sell still will be available, but not on such favorable terms. Seniors want a special offer. They want special terms others don't get. This is an easy way of making that point without having to restructure an entire marketing program.

Compact treadmill burns more calories than jogging!
B. Walk your way to total fitness! Walkmaster II lets you set the pace for effective, whole-body conditioning. Easy-glide fly-wheels and steel rollers offer a smooth workout; sturdy handrails provide safety. Speedometer/odometer monitors speed and progress. Vertical stand provides easy storage. Holds up to 300 lbs.; assembly required. 30"Lx21"Wx40"H. **A776609**, Walkmaster II, **$99.95** or **4 interest-free payments of $25**

(Fig. 6–9) You can see how "As seen on TV" seems to add a documented credential to this exercise machine, described in a catalog mailed to senior citizens.

• *"You could be a big winner!"* Seniors are heavy sweepstakes entrants, so a sweepstakes aimed expressly at seniors should be successful. One caution: The rules and prizes have to be extraordinarily

Eliminate restless tossing & turning
A. Eggcrate® contoured mattress pad helps evenly distribute body weight to relieve sensitive pressure points and provide support for the entire body. ComfortFlow™ ventilation increases and regulates air circulation; helps alleviate heat build-up for a more comfortable sleep. 100% hypoallergenic Biofoam™.
A776476D, Twin mattress pad, **$18.95**
A776492D, Full mattress pad, **$22.95**
A776500D, Queen mattress pad, **$24.95**
A776518D, King mattress pad, **$29.95**

(Fig. 6–10) This item from the same senior-targeted catalog as fig. 6–9 uses "As seen on TV" as a beginning point: "Priced much lower than one seen on TV."

clear. Fig. 6–11 is a sweepstakes for electric scooters. Undoubtedly the secondary prizes are discounts.

"That isn't for me."

Fig. 6–12 is the way an airtour company advertises to the world at large. The heading says, "Australia . . . now even bigger . . . for

(Fig. 6–11) A typical sweepstakes is a legal nightmare and an implementational headache. This specialized sweepstakes promises "Over 80 Winners!" including a monthly drawing. As a lead-generator it outclasses a straight "Send for free details" approach. As a sales closer, it also has weight if the secondary prizes are discounts or accessories.

(Fig. 6–12) The typical senior regards the "outback" look as having nothing in common with him or her. Probably the tour company shares that feeling, because seniors, when mismatched on a tour, can spoil it for the more adventurous.

next winter." This won't win any awards for brilliant copywriting, but notice the picture. Can you imagine seniors responding to this picture? They never can identify with it.

The heading on fig. 6–13 is "Part of the dream." Whose dream? The illustration clarifies, excluding non-seniors. Had the models been younger, the image of a retirement residence would be

(Fig. 6–13) The impression is one of activity. Retirement residences position themselves as active or sedentary, for the dauntless or for the shuffleboard players. Here the illustration clarifies. Notice the major daub of exclusivity: "Join our Ambassador Club Priority Waiting List today. . . ."

muddy. Had they been older, many candidates might feel they're too active for this location.

Demographics Help the Advertiser

Seniors with no children under age 21 living at home are the fastest-growing group of buyers of cameras and camcorders. That should tell marketers something, especially since camcorders are regarded as a complicated piece of equipment.

So if you look at smart advertising for camcorders, you can easily tell which companies are aiming their advertising at seniors. They tie newness to an established base, so the seniors don't feel they've to learn a whole new type of photography.

Tying newness to an established base . . . eliminating the "I can't do that" or the "I'm not one of those people" fears . . . saying to the senior citizens, "This is for you and expressly for you". . . and having seniors agree . . . these techniques are as close to sure-fire as any marketing method to this burgeoning marketplace can be.

Difficult? No. Thoughtful? Yes. As is true of every facet of force-communication, creating effective advertising messages to seniors depends on your ability to form the correct answer to the question: If I were reading this instead of writing it, would it appeal to me?

7

The Mechanics of Advertising

Let's see if we can tie together the mechanical procedures for marketing to seniors in a handful of little rules.

Only the most naive marketer (or is it the most traditional marketer, part of this same group) refuses to acknowledge the emotional *and physical* changes accompanying the aging process.

The most obvious is the deterioration of vision. Easy cataract removal, lens implantation, and radial keratotomy have dented but not significantly changed this problem (unlike Russia, where the prevalence of radial keratotomy means eyeglasses may be obsolete early in the 21st century).

The Easiest, Most Obvious Procedures

Here are some simple-to-implement procedures that can serve you well when selling to this difficult but potentially very profitable group:

For print or mailed advertising . . .

1. No type smaller than 10-point.

This is the most basic of all rules, and I never have understood what logic drives advertisers who aim their messages at older people and set the type in a size so small reading becomes a chore. In fact, if you can, set type no smaller than 12-point. This is easier in a mailing than in a space ad, because a mailing has some elasticity to it whereas a space ad has a finite physical limit. But a warning: Set type smaller than 10-point at your own peril.

(Completeness demands a primitive explanation — under an ancient formula, the height of type is 72 "points" to an inch. So 12-point type — the size of traditional "pica" typewriter typefaces — is ⅙-inch. Ten-point type — the size of "elite" typewriter typefaces — is a bit smaller than ⅐-inch. A 36-point headline is half an inch high. Imagine a senior squinting at 8-point type — ⅑-inch high. It happens all the time.)

Know what? Setting body copy for *any* communication in at least 10-point size is a good idea . . . but an impossible dream, because space limitations of catalogs and space ads may sacrifice type size for information. And that's one of two exceptions to the rule, a necessary trade-off.

The second exception is the physical or psychological circumstance in which *clarifying* explanations require — or seem to require — so much space the only way to include all the words is to set them smaller.

Typically, art directors like to have a lot of space between lines. For easy reading, no more than two points of space, please. Use greater spacing between paragraphs.

2. Response must be easy.

Don't complicate the offer. Simplify the response device (see point 3, following). Every dimension of the communication, from the headline on the ad or brochure to the greeting and especially the p.s. on the letter, has to cater to easy clarity.

Mild warning: Remember that the older people are, the more likely they are to respond by mail instead of by telephone. (Even after years of exposure, some older people fail to recognize an 800 or 888 number as toll-free. The telephone is suspect, anyway, if someone has had a negative telephone sales experience.)

A possible exception, and it's both a subtle exception and an increasingly rare one as people age: For an offer with a highly emotional flavor, including the option of responding by mail might actually *suppress* response. That's because the more emotional the offer, the more an instant response becomes paramount. The time spent filling out a coupon or an order form could result in second thoughts.

3. Include a coupon, with ample room to make entries.

This will make sense to you if you accept the previous point — response must be easy. Inclusion of a coupon almost always enhances response; and here is an interesting phenomenon: When you emphasize a toll-free telephone number and include a coupon, the number of telephone responses also goes up.

For heaven's sake, don't be grudging about the amount of space you allocate to the coupon. Be sure you allow ample room for the individual to print name, address, and other information you require. And if at all possible, include a line saying, "Please print." This instruction, of course, does not apply to the signature you may require for credit card orders.

I've seen response devices challenging the reader so severely that someone who may have decided to buy changes his/her mind at this critical moment.

Even more common is an ad or mailer, a masterpiece of visual clarity . . . with a coupon or response device not only set in tiny type, but not allowing enough room for even a pointillist-artist to inject a name, address, or (far more damaging) a signature.

4. Suggest a discount or bargain.

I simply cannot emphasize enough how valuable this approach is when marketing to seniors. In fact, much of chapter 4 has repeated and glorified this point. An apparent discount has even greater value than an expiration date. Probably you'll want to use the two of them together. A discount can be as simple as, "Made to sell for $100.00; yours for only $69.95." It can be as simple as free coupons (fig. 7–1).

The company mailing these enclosures has separated three groups as specific targets — active adults (fig. 7–2), active seniors (fig. 7–3), and young families. A marketer who uses all three will have — or certainly *should* have — targeted illustrations for each one.

5. *Appear* to appeal to logic.

This may be the most difficult of all the little rules we should follow when marketing to seniors, because if we try to be totally logical we lose the emotional aspect of our appeal. That is why I say,

(Fig. 7–1) Inside this envelope is a batch of offers from various companies, all aimed at the seniors marketplace. The company distributing this mailing has a number of editions; two of them are figs. 7–2 and 7–3, each reaching a segment of the senior marketplace. To the marketer, "marriage mail" offers low-cost distribution of advertising materials: Postage and list costs are split among the participants.

Active
Adults
Edition

Adults 50 to 64 years of age

These ready-to-buy, ready-to-travel consumers are definitely in the prime of their lives. They're fit and financially secure, and they're ready and able to reward themselves – and their families (especially the grandchildren).

For everything from light, low-fat, low-salt foods to special lotions and potions, this is a lucrative market – and the fastest growing demographic grouping in America!

They already dominate product category after category (decaffeinated coffee, women's hair coloring, denture cleansers, etc.), and they're open to all kinds of products and brands that meet their special needs for comfort, security, and personal pleasure.

Quantity/Reach:
17.5 million households nationally (every major trading area)

Market Penetration:
Covers 80% of all households with adults 50-64

Family Size:
Average household size is 2.2

Age Range:
Adults 45-64 primarily (at least one person in the household is between 50 and 64)

Household Income:
Average household income is $31,648

Working Wives:
51% work part/full time

Geographic Location:
Majority live in suburbs, own homes

Coupon Redemption:
87% redeem coupons regularly (72% redeem five or more per week)

Education:
48% graduated from or attended college

Grandparents:
The overwhelming majority spend liberally on gifts for their grandchildren

Mail-responsiveness:
Most are recent responders to a direct-marketing offer

Larry Tucker Targeted Co-op Mailings
188 Broadway, Woodcliff Lake, NJ 07675-9865 • Phone: (201) 307-8888 • FAX: (201) 307-1200

(Fig. 7–2) Congruent with the categorization described in chapter 4, this co-op mailer offers the 50–64 age group as "Active Adults." Marketers know precisely the age group of those receiving their offers — and within this age group, probably the majority are still working.

"Appear to appeal to logic." The ability to apply this rule is the difference between the professional communicator and the dilettante.

6. Don't make a long story short.

Active Seniors Edition

Adults 65 to 75 years of age

This edition reaches to the heart of America's wealthiest generation – home-owning couples with high disposable income, and plenty of time to travel and enjoy the leisure life! Health and quality of life are vitally important to these older consumers, and they spend heavily on vitamins, over-the-counter medications, prescription drugs, retirement services, books, recorded music and a host of other products and services that meet their special needs.

Gardening is popular, and hobbies occupy a good deal of time (for the men, especially). They still play golf, walk and swim for exercise.

Of course, this is the generation that utilizes mail order for so much gift-giving, whether to friends or to family and grandchildren. They're strong supporters of causes and charities, too!

Quantity/Reach:
7.5 million households nationally
(every major trading area)

Market Penetration:
Covers 80% of all households with at least one adult 65-75 years old

Family Size:
Average household size is 2.1

Age Range:
Some have older adults in the home well into their 90s; others have divorced or returned children or grandchildren. Women are 60-75 primarily; male heads of household range from 65-75.

Average Income:
Household income averages $28,437, but most mortgages are paid off

Working Men & Women:
22% of the men and 12% of the women still work at least part time for wages

Geographic Location:
Heavier concentration in the suburbs and small towns; only one-fifth in central cities

Coupon Redemption:
77% use three or more "cents-off" coupons at the grocery or drug store; three-fourths cut and pass along coupons to family and friends

Education:
48% graduated from or attended college

Grandparents:
The overwhelming majority spend liberally for gifts to their grown children, family & grandchildren

Mail-responsiveness:
Most are recent responders to a direct-marketing offer

Larry Tucker Targeted Co-op Mailings
188 Broadway, Woodcliff Lake, NJ 07675-9865 • Phone: (201) 307-8888 • FAX: (201) 307-1200

(Fig. 7–3) This "edition" is "Active Seniors" — the 65–75 age group. Most of these will be retired, or, if still working, comfortable or affluent. The mailer supplies research helping participating marketers to tailor their messages.

I know I said, "Get to the point." But please, please, do *not* interpret this to mean you should condense your story. Seniors not only have more time to absorb the information; they also are more likely to convince themselves slowly instead of reaching an impulse

Turn Senior Names–and Phone Numbers Into Money-Making Leads!

30 Years Mature Market Experience — and a 30,000,000 household file of senior names means that Senior Citizens Unlimited offers your business the largest and most detailed senior list database available.

Our customers include: Financial services; insurance marketers; healthcare providers; hearing instrument dealers; charities; political organizations; eye care centers; adult communities; travel agents; banking services; catalogers; senior publisher networks; fitness and health equipment providers, hearing instrument dealers, adult communities, low cost travel programs, reverse mortgages, mail order apparel, health and beauty aids, LTC facilities, catalogs for in-home shopping and new products for the mature market.

Reach seniors where they live; where they make buying decisions. Senior Citizens Unlimited lists help you get qualified leads, for less money.

Unique features differentiate SCU's Senior Mailing Lists:

- **Exact Age** — 92.4% of all senior names are exact age coded. 76.8% have month and year of birth present for precise age targeting, eliminating the chance of reaching other than the intended audience as can be the case with high percentages of "inferred age" data used by some of our other competitors.

- **Multiple List Sources** — 100% of the senior names and addresses on the SCU masterfile have been verified by two or more independent contributing sources within the past 6 months and 93.5% have three or more contributing sources, providing the highest level of deliverability.

- **Updated Every 120 Days** — SCU's rigorous cross-verification process validates the name, address, and phone number of each record, dropping all non-verified records and deceased individuals.

- **Hotline Names** — 5,627,197 "new senior names" have been added to the file — including fresh response names whose addresses have been verified by another source, individuals turning age 50 in 1995 and households appearing at a new residence.

- **New Movers** — 1,027,256 New Movers — 4.5% of SCU seniors moved into new homes in the past 12 months.

- **FastCounts** — SCU's on-line count system provides you with actual zip counts, not counts based on a sample of the file.

- **ZIP+4 Coding** — SCU provides ZIP+4 coding on your mailing labels to insure that your mail reaches its destination.

- **Telemarketing** — 79.2% of all seniors have current, verified telephone numbers. Phone Numbers cost only 1.5 cents additional per name, with printout of names and addresses, too.

Order Today! Fax your count request to 914-997-8065.
Our sales staff is available from 9:00 am to 5:00 pm E.T. to discuss your senior citizen list needs, do on-line FastCounts and to place your order.
Turnaround within 48 hours after receipt of your label order!

CALL TOLL FREE 1-800-431-1712

(Fig. 7–4) Notice the specifics available to the marketer who rents names from this mailing list. Exquisitely pinpointed selections are available on almost every list from every list company, in this totally computerized era.

decision. Take your time. You may find that a two-page letter works best among the under-45 age group and a four-page letter works best among the over-45 age group. Haste makes waste when marketing to seniors. The only exception is a terse, quick, bulletin-like announcement of "hot, one-of-a-kind" closeout merchandise in which overdescription damages your credibility.

You can see: This last imperative can conflict with the necessity of setting type in at least a 10-point size. Seniors want to be sure they haven't made a mistake by overlooking a detail. Give them details.

> 7. Some dangerous advice: A neatness complex will cost you response.

This is dangerous because no one can claim the point is universally true. The reason for including it here is because neatness causes messages to take on a "standard" look. Neatness is expressed in even balance, and evenly-balanced layouts tend to look the same. Just as marketers are cautioned against generating the same advertising they would aim at Generation-X, so are they cautioned against advertising which seniors may think they already have seen and rejected.

Repetition of messages is a complex issue, because seniors have comfort in what they have seen before. Even more complex: If they've seen it before and rejected it, they're most unlikely to change their minds based on repeated hammering of the same themes.

For renewals . . . don't run on tracks

This is why renewal mailings for periodical subscriptions change their tone with each mailing. They didn't respond to this . . . let's try that. Oh, that didn't get them to renew either? Then we try this. And proof that no group runs on tracks is the result of such marketing.

Some respond to the first mailing and some don't respond until the seventh mailing. We keep mailing until the offer is no longer profitable. And we know, as we mail: Our last shot will be an appeal to the pocketbook . . . something such as, "Look here, my friend, we really do *not* want to lose you. So please accept this special last offer, which we are making to you as proof that we want you to stay with us as a member of our family."

The Validating Enclosure

In a mailing, the most effective way of being sure you've delivered a complete message is to include an extra enclosure — a "validating" enclosure — which covers details, including some you know are inconsequential. Why would you include inconsequential details? Because the reader also recognizes them as inconsequential and thinks, "If they have included information this trivial, they obviously have given me complete details."

This trait, this characteristic, this natural evolutionary process which results from a lifetime of increasing skepticism due to conflicting claims by advertisers . . . and buying products that don't work the way they have been advertised to work . . . and disappointments stemming from items they bought on impulse . . . and newspaper exposés . . . this is the reason longer messages tend to outpull and outsell shorter messages.

Marketers to many demographic groups, but especially to seniors, have embraced a technique of television marketing called the *infomercial*. This, as you can easily determine, is a hybrid word: "Infomercial" is a mixture of information and commercial. The typical infomercial is 30 minutes long. It sells health rejuvenation, investment advice, fishing lures for fishermen to increase their catch, golf clubs, devices to make cooking and baking easier, fund raising, and even the services of a self-professed psychic.

The two keys to infomercials are (1) demonstration and (2) testimonials. Every successful infomercial is peppered with testimonials; when an infomercial fails, chances are the failure is due to insufficient testimonials or poor ones. Testimonials are powerful selling weapons to seniors, especially if they can identify with the person stating a testimonial. That is why a properly-produced infomercial will have its testimonials sprinkled throughout, to convince the viewer to continue to believe the message is true. And that's why an infomercial is so long. Many, many items which have sold successfully through infomercials seem to collapse when advertised in more conventional media.

A Tip for Fund Raising

Good news and bad news. First, good news: As people age, they're more likely to respond to fund-raising appeals (the one exception: appeals from colleges, to which they may have contributed until their own children are of post-college age). Now bad news: They become totally selective in their choice of donations.

This means, first of all, that loyalties carry over, which enables the fund raiser to shorten the time-gap between requests. It means, second, that the mailing or phone call has to say to the senior prospective donor, "This involves *you*. This affects *you*." Pure altruism works poorly on people who may, in fact, reject the entire premise of any appeal.

So the fund raiser's alertness and adeptness has to drive the appeal to "cold lists" of seniors. Their automatic question, "Am I my brother's keeper?" has to be answered, "Yes, you are, because this person *is* your brother . . . and your brother may one day be you."

The technique of bestowing psychological awards — appointment to an "Advisory Board," for example — is an excellent technique for holding seniors in the donor group. Loyalty exists, but loyalty of any type is fragile. Be sure to remind the senior contributor of that loyalty with each contact.

Two formats seem to be working well in the late 1990s. One is the "Snap-Pak." Snap-Paks have a perforation along one edge. The recipient snaps the package open by tearing along the perforation. The other is the "Speed Format" (fig. 7–5). If you're involved in fund raising, consider these formats, which have rescued a number of mailers who had great difficulty raising funds with mailings using conventional envelopes.

Personalization Availabilities

Seniors aren't alone in availabilities of list selection and special mailing packages. Almost every identifiable demographic group with any buying power is accessible to marketers.

Fig. 7–6 is the first page of a single-insertion source of advertising to seniors. Note: This is page one of *50* pages.

(Fig. 7–5) This is a bulk mail envelope, but who can resist opening it? Because an unopened envelope can destroy the most brilliant message inside it, "speed formats" such as this are worth testing. Most direct mail printers have a proprietary speed format available.

SENIOR ADS, U.S.A. 1-800-55-SENIOR
P.O. BOX 600600, SAN DIEGO, CA 92160

January 9, 1995

FREQ	NEWSPAPERS/MAGAZINES	METHOD OF DISTRIBUTION	READERS	MINIMUM SIZE	1/4 PAGE COST	1/2 PAGE COST	FULL PAGE COST	PAPER SIZE
	ALABAMA							
M*	Registered Nurses (Nursing Matters)	DM	75,000	896	896	1326	2210	9 7/8" x 13"
W*>	Senior Birmingham Health & Fitness (Health & Fitness)	DM	565,000	616	3388	6696	13396	13" x 21 3/4"
M*>	Senior Ft Payne (Senior Lifestyles)	DM/PS	19,000	196	294	587	1174	12 3/4" x 21 1/2"
M*	Senior Southern Alabama (60+ News)	PT	32,500	306	470	917	1833	10 1/4" x 13"
BM	Senior Tennessee Valley (Golden Gazette)	DM	37,500	189	188	366	729	10 1/4" x 13 1/2"
M	Senior Tuscaloosa (Senior Edition)	DM/PT/PS	30,875	200	133 (3X ONLY)	266	532	10 5/16" x 13"
	ALASKA							
M	American Legion (Sane)	DM	22,322	200	350	700	1400	9 11/16" x 14'
BM	Car & Travel Magazine (Sane)	DM/PS	14,028	698	1/3~231	1397	2328	7" x 9 3/4"
M*	Senior Anchorage (Senior Voice)	DM	17,500	194	194	378	748	9 3/4" x 15 3/4"
	ARKANSAS							
BM*	AAA Midwest Motorist Mag (Sane (AARXMO))	DM/PS	892,862	800	1/2~3040	4400	8002	7" x 9 1/2"
Q	American Legion (Sane)	DM	85,000	200	400	800	1600	10 7/8" x 16"
M	Senior Arkansas (Active Years)	PT/DM	125,000	334	587	846	1276	10" x 12 3/4"
M*	Senior Greater Arkansas (Aging Arkansas)	DM	102,500	275	275	502	980	10 1/3" x 16"
M	Senior Lakes Region (Senior Living)	PT/DM	75,150	242	362	661	792	10" x 15 1/2"
M*	SeniorMountain Home (Senior Focus)	DM/PS	26,250	208	208	420	813	10 1/16" x 12 1/2"
BM	Senior NW Arkansas (Senior Living)	PT/DM	62,500	231	297	462	737	10" x 15 1/2"

(Fig. 7–6) If you think media opportunities are limited, this should disabuse you of that notion. Shown here is page one of a 50-page listing of local senior publications. This is exclusive of national periodicals, targeted broadcasts, and a multitude of senior-aimed Internet sites.

Fig. 7–7 is an example of "selective binding": The card was bound into an issue of *Modern Maturity*. With today's technology, this is primitive selective binding. Automobile manufacturers, for example, can personalize their reference to the subscriber's individual automobile.

Figs. 7–8a and 7–8b are the front and back of a mylar "marriage mail" packet. Within this packet is a group of cards, each one of which sells a product aimed at seniors — pharmaceuticals, exercise machines, hearing aids, even a poem for the grandchild.

NEW FOR AARP MEMBERS!

Yes, please rush me my FREE information kit and personalized quote.

☐ **AARP Permanent Life**   ☐ **AARP Level Premium Term Life**

RUTH MOFFETT
YOUR RATES FOR AARP PERMANENT LIFE INSURANCE WILL NEVER BE LOWER. CALL OR RETURN THIS CARD BEFORE

APRIL 23, 1996
TO LEARN HOW YOU CAN SAVE ON PREMIUMS.

Name_____

Address_____

City/State/Zip_____

Date of Birth_____/_____/_____

Telephone (_____)_____

AARP Membership No._____

Social Security No. (Optional)____-____-____

002A Work ☐ Full Time ☐ Part Time ☐ Retired

CODE C13002 N

Spouse's Name_____

Date of Birth_____/_____/_____

Social Security No. (Optional)____-____-____

Work ☐ Full Time ☐ Part Time ☐ Retired

For faster service, call toll free
1-800-449-1517
8am to 8pm (EST) Monday–Friday.

***AARP* Life Insurance Program**
NEW YORK LIFE
5505 West Cypress, Tampa, FL 33607-1707

(Fig. 7–7) Bound into an issue of a magazine is this personalized card. Contemporary technology has made possible better typography, messages more matched to the individual, and individualized imprints onto advertising pages.

(Figs. 7–8a and 7–8b) This is the front and back of a "marriage mail" card packet. Note the participants . . . and the common factor — retirement.

Conclusion

Reaching seniors *as seniors* is much in order, with one caveat: If the individual feels he or she is being patronized, forget it.

With readable typefaces, coupons with their offer clearly stated, and loyalty rewards and reminders, success is far more certain than it would be for the marketer who simply sends out mail or runs advertising.

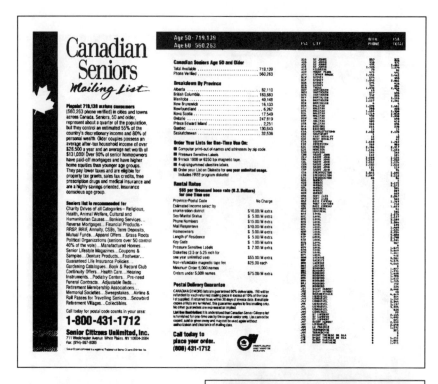

(Fig. 7–9) Here is just the beginning of a Canadian seniors list, available with many sub-selections.

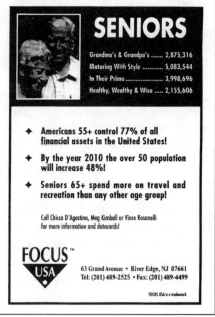

(Fig. 7–10) This is one of many space ads for lists of senior names, placed in marketing publications.

8

AARP — Its Pros and Cons

The American Association of Retired Persons is arguably the most influential private organization in the world.

Without argument, it is the most influential not-for-profit organization in the world. (Political parties are "for profit," aren't they?) No one would argue that it's America's most powerful special interest lobbyist.

The AARP bellwether publication, *Modern Maturity*, and the tabloid newsprint publication *AARP News Bulletin* at presstime each claimed more than 56 million readers. (This optimistic number coincides with the total number of over-50s.)

Optimistic or not, *Modern Maturity* has far and away the highest circulation of any consumer magazine — upward of 20 million copies. At this writing, a page in color is priced at well above $200,000. (Full pages aren't available in the newspaper-style *AARP News Bulletin*. A half-page, in black and white, costs more than $170,000.)

Compare those with a page in *Mature Outlook*, a parallel publication not affiliated with a national not-for-profit group. A black-and-white page in *Mature Outlook* costs about $30,000. Cheaper? In total cost, yes. Per person reached, no. *Mature Outlook* has a circulation of about 2,000,000. That translates into $15 per thousand. With its 36 million circulation, *Modern Maturity*, at $212,000, costs less than $6 per thousand.

(You probably know this. The general rule is: The smaller the circulation, the higher the cost per thousand. Generalizations aren't always true. *Longevity*, which at presstime has a circulation of about 850,000, has a black-and-white page rate of $7558 — only about $9 per thousand.)

As chapter 10 points out, the influence of AARP and *Modern Maturity* can only grow. With 76 million "baby boomers" joining the over-50 ranks between 1996 and 2002, both influence and circulation will be even more formidable than they've been in the past.

(A curiosity: *Modern Maturity* advises its advertisers — wisely — to use larger type. In late 1995, the magazine itself reduced the size of its text face from 11-point Times Roman to 9.25-point Stone Serif. This was the result of a recommendation by a consultant who, according to *Folio:*, the magazine for magazine publishers, said the larger size "looks like it's for a kid. We didn't want to treat readers as 'infirm.'" In anticipation of its incoming readership, the magazine is aiming itself more toward the 50-to-60 age group; the over-60 loyalties are firmly in place.

Can You Get an
AARP Recommendation?

Anticipate two circumstances, if you want to reach the huge AARP membership through advertising in either *Modern Maturity* or *AARP News Bulletin:*

First, you'll encounter the standard classic response you can expect from any publication that's the leader in its field: "Being in the magazine automatically adds the AARP patina to what you're advertising. A direct endorsement? Neither logical nor possible."

Second, if what you're advertising is competitive with any AARP proprietary products or services — such as prescriptions,

Whose lips wear 1/3*
of the lipstick?

It's on the lips of women 50+. They buy one in every three lipsticks.
And they buy the foundation and moisturizer to go with it.
If you're suffering from share shock, talk lipstick to 50+. Call up Steve Alexander
at Modern Maturity, 212-599-1880, and up your share!

**Modern Maturity.
A new face.
A new voice.
A new market.**

(Fig. 8–1) Intended to recruit advertisers, this ad may not reflect the actual editorial philosophy of a publication aimed at seniors. As "baby boomers" turn 50, they seldom regard themselves as having crossed a permanent border into a realm they would have to share with "the elderly." Senior discounts are regarded as perks; senior appellations are regarded as premature.

insurance or travel — be prepared to be turned down cold. *Modern Maturity* won't accept competitive advertising.

Should you appeal to AARP members as AARP members?

With all the senior lists at hand, why try to reach AARP members *as* AARP members through advertising in the pages of one of its publications?

The answer is the cachet the organization radiates to many of its members. AARP is a powerful lobbyist, spending millions to promote or oppose legislation affecting its membership.

But we all know that lobbying and militating for federal, state, and local privileges is a generic icon, not likely to inspire either loyalty or renewed membership. In real benefits, AARP has struck agreements with many vendors, ranging from hotels and motels to car rentals and theme park admissions, resulting in discounts for those who flash the well-known AARP membership card.

Power Behind the Throne

AARP casts a giant shadow. A 21-year-old was quoted in a national magazine:

"The AARP has the power to mortgage our future. Our generation is under attack."

Overstated, to be sure. But much of AARP's marketing power stems from international realization of its political power.

When Ronald Reagan was president of the United States, AARP was credited with killing a law that would have insured people against catastrophic illness. Critics claimed AARP's opposition was based on the organization's fear that such a national measure would damage AARP's own giant insurance program.

(And giant it is. AARP doesn't actually write its own insurance, but some of the biggest companies in the nation are its insurance partners. For example, at presstime Prudential writes AARP's group health insurance; Hartford writes auto and homeowners; Foremost handles mobile homes; and New York Life is the company for life insurance. The size of AARP's policyholder-potential and political

clout is such that none of these companies would risk the relationship by advertising parallel coverage outside the AARP orbit.)

Examples of various types of AARP insurance are figs. 8–2
through 8–5.

Whether because of criticism or because of a change in attitude
and of proposed legislation, in recent years AARP has supported in-
suring the aged against extravagantly-priced long-term care. Again,
detractors find a reason to criticize, suggesting this is because AARP
suffers defections when it becomes too self-serving.

AARP As a Self-Advertiser

Like many giants aware of their power, AARP is cautious in its
own advertising.

For example, its advertising for life insurance doesn't claim
"Better Rates"; it claims "Competitive Rates." The approach is one
of exclusivity rather than greed — "At last there's life insurance

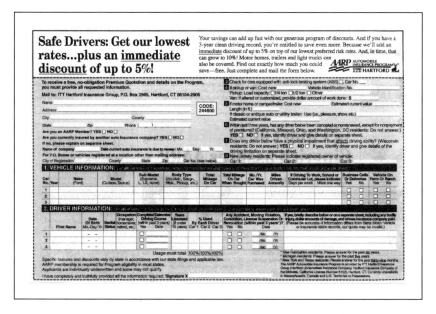

(Fig. 8–2) AARP automobile insurance is handled by ITT Hartford.

5 reasons why our new Life Insurance Program makes such good sense for AARP members!

1. Affordable, quality life insurance designed for people age 50 plus.

AARP has selected New York Life Insurance Company to offer its new Life Insurance Program. If you're an AARP member age 50 to 80, it's easy to apply; there's no physical exam, just three health questions to answer. And members' spouses age 45 and older are also eligible.

2. The coverage you want at a price you can afford.

Coverage of up to $25,000 is available. And you can choose from several term or permanent products, including those described here. Whether you're seeking to maximize family protection or minimize premium costs, this Program has a product for you.

3. More value for your premium dollar.

Among the Program's special features are a *waiver of premium for nursing home confinement*, plus a *living benefit*, which provides for

immediate access to half the benefit amount if an insured is diagnosed with a terminal illness. (Further details on these features — plus facts on costs, eligibility, renewability, limitations and exclusions — are included in the Program's free information kit, which you can request by phone or mail.)

AARP PERMANENT LIFE

Permanent group coverage that can help build a nest egg for your survivors, or offset the impact of final expenses and funeral costs. Available to AARP members 50–80. Premiums are expected to remain level while policy is in force. May be kept to age 100, then cashed in for the full benefit amount.

AARP LEVEL PREMIUM TERM LIFE

Coverage that's ideal for short term needs, such as paying off mortgages or other obligations that may decrease over time. Available to members 50–64. Premiums are expected to remain level; benefit amount will decline at five-year attained age intervals. May be kept to age 75, then converted to a permanent policy.

4. Offered by New York Life.

New York Life has earned the highest possible ratings from Moody's for financial strength, A.M. Best for financial stability, and Standard & Poor's and Duff & Phelps for claims paying ability.

5. A free information kit and a free quote.

Find out how to protect *your* family better. For your free kit, plus a free personalized quote, complete and return the attached card or call toll free:

1-800-449-1517

8:00 am to 8:00 pm (Eastern Time) Monday–Friday. You can also call for details on other products offered through the Program.

AARP Life Insurance Program
NEW YORK LIFE

5505 West Cypress, Tampa, FL 33607-1707

The AARP Life Insurance Program is underwritten by New York Life Insurance Company, New York, NY 10010. AARP membership is required for Program eligibility. Specific products not available in all states. CODE C13002N

(Fig. 8–3) AARP life insurance is handled by New York Life.

designed especially for AARP members" — a semi-claim that leans hard on the assumed prestige and image of the organization itself.

The auto and homeowners insurance programs advertise themselves as "designed especially for AARP Members." Nowhere does the advertising (or a buckslip enclosed with AARP literature) claim

(Fig. 8–4) AARP health insurance is handled by Prudential.

lowest rates. The closest any claim comes to superiority is actually "parity advertising" — a standard technique in which the claim of equality is couched in words the reader may interpret as a claim of superiority: "The Homeowners Program lets you choose from a range of coverages second to none."

The Pharmacy Service invites members (all these services are, obviously, for members only) to "save money." No claim is made for lowest prices; it's "low prices."

A commercial competitor, U.S. Senior Health Care Association, Inc., has a box on its reply device: "Yes, I would like to see how

(Fig. 8–5) AARP mobile home insurance is handled by Foremost.

I can become a member of USSHCA and save BIG on prescription drugs." Capitalizing the word "BIG" is, at least as of now, a promotional move AARP regards as too aggressive.

Competitively, the major advantage AARP has over its for-profit rivals is the extraordinary faith the many millions of AARP

(Fig. 8–6) AARP sells prescriptions to its members by mail. Discount pharmacies often advertise themselves as being "below AARP prices."

members place in the organization. Even the most casual member recognizes the power any group which ostensibly speaks for more than 30 million members can wield.

Arrogant or not, difficult to deal with or not, autocratic or not, the American Association of Retired Persons has benefited senior citizens far beyond the capability of any other organization. In state after state, it has beaten down taxes. On the national level, it has militated for maintaining and increasing senior benefits.

In the private sector, AARP has arranged discounts from hotels, motels, car rental companies, and tour operators. It offers membership in a motor club. It has a co-branded credit card. All these are immensely successful, not only because of the organization's size but also because member trust is so high.

Politicians know the power of AARP. They respect it and respond to it.

In the 21st century, a natural evolutionary process might have a competing organization either splinter off or be formed by dissi-

(Fig. 8–7) AARP offers its members an annuity program, through American Maturity Life.

(Fig. 8–8) AARP has appointed Scudder to implement a "no-fee AARP IRA" (individual retirement account) investment program for its members.

dent AARP officials. Whether or not this happens, seniors know they're organized . . . and organized groups have political, social, and economic power.

"Edgar can't come to the phone right now...
He's busy making our home our castle."

If it's true that people improve with age, so do their homes.

In fact, studies show that people over 50 are just as likely to invest in home furnishings and remodeling as any other age group.

To improve matters, Modern Maturity (read by nearly half of all mature Americans) will furnish you with a very practical way to reach them.

(Figs. 8–9, 8–10, 8–11) These are three of a series of ads AARP runs in advertising magazines for its magazine, *Modern Maturity*.

"When we hit one hundred miles,
let's stop for a bite."

People over 50 have been around the block a few
times. In fact, they're more likely than their under-50
counterparts to walk at least 10 miles a week.

The people who take such pleasure in walking
(and in the athletic shoes they wear) hit their stride
with Modern Maturity, the magazine read by nearly
half of them.

9

The Do's and Don'ts of Telemarketing

Anybody can answer the phone. Anybody can make a phone call."

Marketers who take this position suffer from lack of information. And whose fault is it that they suffer from lack of information? Why don't they have better information on the difference between sophisticated, profitable, non-intrusive telemarketing and somebody answering the phone?

Actually, telemarketing is a much more precise and more disciplined profession than placing ads and buying media. Do telemarketers say to advertising agency production people and media directors, "Anybody can set type and buy space ads and broadcast time"?

Some of the Bloom Is Off the Rose

A mistake some telemarketers make is assuming the medium drives the message. It used to be that way; but aggressive telemarketing is not only in disrepute; some states have straitjacket legislation governing it. And one reason for the legislation is complaints by seniors that they were "tricked" into buying something they didn't want.

No question about it, some of the bloom is off the telemarketing rose. But no question about it, the medium has plenty of juice left in it . . . if handled professionally and without duplicity. In fact, such developments as predictive dialing have made telemarketing far more efficient than it was in telemarketing's "Golden Decade" — 1970 to 1980.

The Two Faces of Telemarketing

If it's news to any marketer that two principal types of telemarketing exist — inbound and outbound — that marketer has been lost in a time warp.

But it may be news that these two types of telemarketing are identical only in the instrument used and the end result desired.

Inbound telemarketing, on a toll-free line (if it isn't toll-free, forget it as far as seniors are concerned), entails three demands: 1) total patience; 2) total familiarity with what's being sold; 3) total determination to upsell.

Faxed and couponed orders have an advantage in that they can't be misunderstood or mistranslated; but upselling is difficult, because upselling an order that comes into a business without a personal contact requires the superimposition of that personal contact *after the fact* — which means exposure to that deadly syndrome, Buyer's Remorse.

In simpler terms: You call the originator of a faxed order to confirm the order. Fine. Then you try to upsell. Maybe it's a go . . . maybe it's a no-go . . . and maybe you kill the order altogether, because 1) anywhere from 10 minutes to a day have elapsed since the order was faxed; 2) the customer may not like your telephone voice; 3) the customer may sense he or she is being "pitched," which is a turn-off; 4) any time-split in a selling situation brings emphasis to the negatives, not the positives.

Telemarketing's scarlet letter

Telemarketing bears a cross no other medium carries — not television, not the Internet, not talk radio, No, it isn't a cross, it's a letter of the alphabet — the label "I" for *intrusiveness*. This latter-day scarlet letter carries a "be careful" warning to reckless telemarketers who use the same technique they used in the 1970s — the "How are *you* today?" opening, followed by an intense sales pitch. Some carryover naifs still respond to pressure, but Buyer's Remorse is rampant, second thoughts cause cancellations and refusals, and legislation pulls the canine teeth of such outdated methods.

The "P.I." Deal and Other Telemarketing Profit Centers

Here's the quandary: It's unlikely that even though the industry is amassing an ungodly amount of editorial scar tissue, telemarketing is about to disappear . . . or even diminish.

Why? Because telemarketing has almost no commercial history other than success. The question isn't whether telemarketing produces results, but how much.

(In the Golden Decade, telemarketers anticipated a 200 percent to 300 percent increase in sales.)

From a marketing point of view, an advertiser usually can negotiate with one or another telemarketing company to exploit a competitive area in which telephone salespeople have an edge over other media. Telemarketing quite naturally qualifies for the "P.I. Deal."

P.I. means per inquiry. Instead of paying a flat amount of money whether the campaign works or not, the advertiser takes almost no risk. What advertiser can resist this? The cost is based on the number of leads the campaign generates.

The reason I say "almost" no cost is because the advertiser typically underwrites at least some of the setup costs. And the advantage to the marketer is obvious: By partnering in these costs, the advertiser can have a say in what's included in the script, excluded from the script, and subject to controlled ad libs. Individual salespeople, working on commission, tend to depart from the script. (By the time the consumer has complained and demanded a refund, they also have departed from the company: Turnover can be 500 percent to 600 percent per year.)

P.I. deals are certainly not new. Radio stations, for example, have been offering P.I. deals for at least 60 years. But again telemarketers have a P.I. edge: Radio stations typically offer the poorest time periods they can't sell any other way. Telemarketers do their best job between six p.m. and nine p.m. weekdays and all day Saturday and Sunday — the very best time periods, whether they're on a P.I. deal or not.

Not for Every Product or Service

An "if" factor relates to what you're selling to seniors. If the campaign is to generate store traffic for a food staple, be cautious. That isn't telemarketing's strength. Seniors react to the "deal in hand," and the spoken word carries another anvil in its rucksack: It doesn't include a coupon or printed evidence. (Mailing coupons or verification after the fact is weak.) If the campaign is for subscriptions . . . or test driving an automobile . . . or a political candidate . . . or an insurance estimate . . . or offering new services to existing customers . . . or a free trial of anything at all . . . telemarketing has top credentials. Telemarketing can't lose. In such circumstances it's the surest media bet an advertiser has.

The Difference Between Inbound and Outbound

The term "telemarketing" straddles the two different universes, inbound and outbound. These two facets of telemarketing have only one marker in common: the telephone itself.

Be cautious about lumping inbound and outbound together when planning a telemarketing campaign. The difference in expertise, staffing, and mechanisms of these two separate businesses can be considerable.

Not all inbound is toll-free, but everybody in advertising knows the benefit of a toll-free number, especially when asking seniors to call. If you don't have a toll-free number or a local number *and* no phone company per-call charge, two words of advice when suggesting the reader of an ad or recipient of a piece of mail make that inbound call: Forget it. Seniors won't call a number that costs them money, to order something they didn't want before they saw or heard your message.

In fact, unless you emphasize heavily: "For fastest service call right now" or "Don't take a chance of missing out. Call to be sure you get . . ." or "special bonus if you call before 10 p.m.," the telephone — the instrument that has betrayed them in the past and about whose abuses they've read so much — will sit on the table, unused.

Training someone to accept inbound calls and to upsell — gently, please — takes little time. The inbound telemarketer doesn't have to generate the original desire to buy, and that's a gigantic difference between inbound and outbound.

Outbound is a different game altogether. Equipment is far more sophisticated. Terminology differs. Training and setup can take days, and turning telemarketers loose without monitoring the first half-day's calls is close to suicidal. Refine, refine, refine — this approaches scientific studies.

Outbound employee turnover is far higher. Legal problems, including those stemming from operator ad-libs and operator disenchantment, can haunt you. Calls have to be clustered within a limited number of hours.

The bugaboo of litigation

Seniors are favorite targets of lawyers who know that when an elderly person claims he or she has been defrauded, juries tend to believe. So suits against telephone sales groups are more prevalent than they are against any other type of advertising. Perception is: "Oh, this guy is a telemarketer. Rule against him."

Outbound is an iffy business, and any level short of total 100 percent professionalism is going to lead to potential disaster. The marketer who cavalierly says, "Anybody can talk on the telephone," can face not only immediate legal problems, but the ancillary problems stemming from untargeted sales appeals, personnel not dedicated to this job, poor record-keeping, slow transfer of data to the order department, and the worst of all results: a situation in which an actually eager prospect is killed off.

So the telemarketer should begin the conversation with total sincerity: "I'm Martin Johnston. I'm calling on behalf of the Senior Discount Division of Arizona Pharmaceutical Company." Not — "Hello, Mrs. Hoffman? How are you today?"

If a marketer is unable to equate the high per-contact cost of telemarketing with a high rate of results, the medium is wrong for whatever he or she is selling. No question: Next to an in-person call, telemarketing is the most expensive of all media. Approaching it in an amateur manner, without thoroughly scripted and thoroughly tested approaches, will waste both money and prospects.

Calling Seniors:
Avoid Casual Unprofessionalism

Seniors *detest* being called by their first name, by someone whose voice betrays youth. Yet a ridiculous number of scripted telemarketing openings call for the first name. Suggestion: Don't do that. You can achieve equivalence as the pitch progresses. Don't risk irritating an individual who resents familiarity from the unfamiliar.

The equations couldn't be simpler: Following the rules equals professionalism. Ignoring the rules equals amateurism.

That goes for the telephone voice, too. Here we have yet another area in which the telemarketer carries a burden: Lawsuits from would-be operators.

I'm puzzled that the same marketer who won't make a space-buy without getting half a ton of information about demographics, psychographics, and circulation thinks telemarketing doesn't require expertise. So even if that marketer decides to go ahead with telemarketing, he turns the program over to a junior writer or assumes he can do it himself.

Is this Mrs. John Jones? It is? Mrs. Jones, how are you today?

If ever a sentence were deadly, that's it: "How are you today?" My wife has a standard answer — on those rare occasions when she doesn't hang up. She'll say, "Oh, dreadful, dreadful. The dog died. Yes, the dog died. You see, he was in the barn when it caught fire. I hated to see that barn catch fire, but it happened when flames spread from the house. It wasn't my fault. When I shot that burglar, the kick from the shotgun broke my arm and I fell back against the table. The candle fell on the floor and started the fire. I couldn't put out the candle because my arm was broken, and you probably know I lost my other arm in that accident at the factory. I wish the car hadn't been parked in the driveway, next to that gasoline drum." And she goes on until the caller hangs up.

I propose that readers of this book *not* hang up on that "How are you today?" opening because we should stay abreast of what telemarketers are doing. (My tennis partner isn't so kind. A man's voice said, "Hi, how are you today?" and he hung up. It turned out to be a friend trying to put together a tennis game.)

A rapier, not a shotgun

Among nonprofessionals the most expensive pitfall is making random calls to anyone in the pile of prospect names. A professional telemarketer knows if you're making outbound calls, you call just "the tip of the pyramid." Once you start dipping down into the middle of the pile, you're in dangerous territory.

The tip of the pyramid means you call only the best prospects. Using telemarketing for "shotgun" prospecting doesn't make any more business sense than a doctor treating every patient for malaria, whether that patient has any symptoms or not.

Telemarketing uses a rapier, not a shotgun. We choose a target and with an exquisitely delicate thrust stab it right through the wallet. Telemarketing should observe the First Great Law of Force-Communication, because violations of that law are more costly in telemarketing than in any other medium:

Reach and influence, at the lowest possible cost, the most people who can and will buy what you have to sell.

The telemarketer's job is to convert that *academic* understanding into a *force-communication* understanding. Every word of that law makes sense to the telemarketer.

Telemarketing guarantees absolute reach. If you run an ad in a publication or a broadcast campaign, no matter how sophisticated your market research might be you have only the vaguest idea of whether or not you've reached your targets. With telemarketing, the moment that person picks up the phone — whether to call you or to take your call — you know you've reached him or her.

Don't ignore the words "and influence." This means getting to the point, with clarity. An absolute canon: Specifics sell. Generalizations don't sell.

The middle phrase, "at the lowest possible cost," eliminates outbound calls to people in the lower sections of the pyramid. If those people want to call *in*, that's gravy. In fact, make it as easy and as profitable as possible to have them call in. Why? Because once they've called in they join that select group at the top of the pyramid and it's both logical and profitable to contact them.

Now look at the last phrase: It isn't "the most people"; it's "the most people who can and will buy what you have to sell." That phrase alone should say to you: Gold is in those stones you've shoveled out of the river of inquiries. Are you following up multi-buyers with special telephone offers?

The selectivity suggested in chapter 3 not only is a good criterion for choosing which seniors are the most people who can and will buy what you have to sell; it's a mandatory criterion for outbound telemarketing. Countless unsuccessful telemarketers blame the medium for failure; no, failure stems from their own inability to isolate the proper individuals.

That inability kills the other component of the First Great Law: "at the lowest possible cost." *Is* telemarketing the way to reach them at the lowest possible cost? Or is telemarketing, *as a reinforcement*, the way to reach them at the lowest possible cost? Testing brings the answers.

Certainly if you have a continuity program or a subscription-based publication, telemarketing can be the instrument for reviving drop-outs. But don't ruin the medium for others: Two-call maximum, please — the first is a friendly "I know you don't want to miss this" and the second is "We're just in time." Hammering beyond that does no damage in direct mail; it cements a negative attitude toward the medium as a whole in telemarketing.

Be Ready to Answer Questions

Don't go rushing out with a telemarketing campaign until you, or some experienced supervisors, have tested the approach through a number of calls.

Some prospects will have questions. Note them, script them, and include them in the total package. Answers to questions should be at the elbow of every telemarketer. Professional telemarketing companies may have 100 or more possible questions, available to the operator on the computer screen by a quick key-tap of a word.

A question that isn't on the list should be handled carefully: "That's a question I hadn't thought of, and I really don't know the answer. Tell you what: I'll have Joe Gilbert, our vice president, call you back. Joe knows everything about this company." That sets up a call-back instead of a potentially lost sale.

Telemarketing as an Ancillary

In a direct marketing campaign, adding inbound telemarketing can be as easy as adding a couple of lines of type to the coupon or response device . . . or to the p.s. of a letter.

A typical weak p.s. on a letter: "Don't you agree this is a wonderful and unique opportunity? I urge you to respond without delay because delay can be costly to you."

Compare that with a telemarketing p.s.: "To take advantage of this special private discount, be sure to mail the postage-free card or call my personal toll-free phone number within the next 10 days. I'd hate to see you miss out."

For many advertisers, tacking a toll-free number onto every mass communication, including television commercials, has become automatic. You never know when the impulse to buy will strike.

Case history: insurance

Telemarketing quite regularly has been showing a 40 percent lift for insurance products.

Insurance companies have the same problem outbound telemarketing companies have: Companies with agents, if those agents aren't doing business, have a heavy turnover. So they say to their marketing departments, "Get us an ongoing supply of leads." Companies selling by mail usually already are using the phone to qualify or close. But to qualify or close *whom?* The message to the advertising agencies or marketing departments: "Keep those leads coming in or our superstructure collapses."

A flood of advertising begins. Newspapers, magazines, radio, television, direct response, online, fixed position media . . . all get their share. Why not telemarketing?

Why exclude the medium that has three benefits going for it? First, it's the most flexible of all media. Clients can expand or shrink their campaigns literally in hours. Second, it delivers the hottest and most qualified leads of all media. And third, telemarketing has proved it can deliver insurance leads at a more than competitive cost.

(But can you imagine the chaos if every insurance company had a battery of telemarketers ringing up consumers and asking, "How are you today?") If the medium is to remain viable, not just for insurance but for any approach to lapsed buyers or non-customers, the message has to be matched not just to the medium but to the specific circumstance . . . and to the specific target. Levity and in-talk and humor may work for *Spin* and *Wired* magazines. They don't work when trying to convince seniors to buy.

The Logic

Telemarketing can justify itself on several levels:

- Follow-up calls to answer questions
- Special timely offers
- Testing programs before investing heavily in other media
- The ability to respond (and better yet, change the sales argument — instantly)
- Surveys and information-gathering
- Immediacy
- Cross-selling and upselling

Any one of these justifies including telemarketing in the budget. But an ongoing imperative: *Use telemarketing logically.*

Getting attention is not parallel to offering a benefit. So the telemarketer who pays more attention to getting attention than to why he or she is supposed to be getting attention won't enjoy the success this medium might offer.

Telemarketing isn't for every product, or every service, or every fund-raising venture. It makes sense when intelligent minds conclude that those who hear the message should respond . . . and then implement that conclusion with an intelligent, fully-scripted campaign targeted at the proper groups of seniors.

A little rule that helps

In marketing, asking questions can help formulate attitudes. Read that sentence a couple of times and you can see another bene-fit of the medium: It's implicitly target-involving.

Telemarketers who don't ask questions beyond "How are you today?" are losing a powerful weapon. And the questions that matter, as attitude-formulators, aren't about name and address and age range. They're cleverly-constructed questions that *seem to be* seeking opinions but actually are helping form those opinions.

The way an experienced telemarketer frames the question validates the rule. The question helps form a *positive* attitude. The most personal of all mass media justifies its existence.

Solo or in Concert?

Telemarketing can succeed as the only medium of force-communication, provided you reach the right group of seniors with the right message. That's another truism. (And add to the mix: The right voice making the presentation.) But potent synergism exists when you combine telemarketing with direct mail. One plus one equals three. Direct mail *plus* telemarketing, to limited universes, has invariably brought considerably more response than either medium alone, far in excess of the additional cost.

This doesn't apply to space and broadcast advertising. Why? Because the telemarketer can refer to the mailing; generate guilt when the recipient admits — either to the telemarketer or to himself/herself — that the mail has gone unread; and start up the engine of enthusiasm by formulating an attitude based on questions about the mailing. "I didn't see that" is a guiltless rejoinder to a question about a space ad or television spot.

The greatest caution for a telemarketer is recognizing both the potential and the limitations of the medium and working within those borders while avoiding a "Promise whatever you have to promise to get the deal" attitude.

Whatever you do in telemarketing, a favor, please: Don't start the conversation with "How are you today?"

10

After 2010 What?

Seniors are going to dominate the 21st century.

Modern Maturity easily could reach a circulation of 35 million by 2010. By the magazine's estimate of 2.67 readers per copy, that's more than 93 million readers.

That incredible number isn't as big a jump as it might seem to be. By 2010 the percentage of over-50s will increase to close to 100 million — a jump of about 49 percent. The under-50s? Anticipation is growth of less than one percent.

So forget about thinking of seniors as a niche market. Not only will seniors comprise the biggest identifiable demographic group, by far; seniors will — as they already do — control more spending power than any other group, by far.

For the marketer, the new crop of seniors (the postwar "baby boomers") is ideal. They are direct mail responsive. They are less worried about being on a fixed income than the first identifiable group (born between 1915 and 1940). They welcome advertising with an "exclusivity" or "convenience" thrust more than any other group, even including the pre-Generation-Xers. And they have money.

In fact, according to Robert Perlstein, head of database/media company Lifestyle Change Communications, seniors already command considerably more than $1 *trillion* in spending power. The 55–64 group has the highest per-capita income. The over-65s have the most discretionary income.

With this lucrative pot simmering away, will marketers have a more difficult time convincing seniors to spend on *their* offers?

Probably.

Two reasons for this. First: Awareness of the overavailability of competing sources, each one claiming "I have something for you because you're you," may have come slowly. But it's there now, ringing loudly to warn companies with something to sell to this group. Invariably when competitors clamor for attention and dollars, the noise becomes more and more strident and the target backs away.

Second: Attention spans are shorter than they ever have been, but, as Al Jolson used to say, you ain't seen nothin' yet. The standard way to seize attention is to scream. Imagine a marketplace in which every vendor screams. Bedlam. The occasional respite of sweet reason may pass unnoticed in the pandemonium.

Which Motivators Will Survive?

Exclusivity will continue to work . . . *if the advertiser can convince the senior that this really is exclusive.* Convenience will work . . . *if the advertiser can convince the senior that this really is convenient.* Pleasure will work . . . *if the advertiser can convince the senior that this really will bring pleasure.*

And in each case, the ability to convince will be tied more and more to the ability to gain attention in the first place.

How about the more traditional motivators — fear, greed, guilt, need for approval?

Fear still will have power, but as (see chapter 3) the fixed income group becomes less fearful of running out of money, fear will have to be aimed more at the physical aspects of life than at loss of lifestyle.

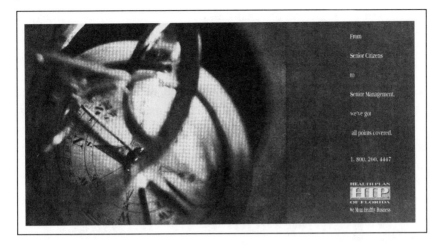

From
Senior Citizens
to
Senior Management.
we've got
all points covered.

1. 800. 260. 4447

HEALTH PLAN
HIP
OF FLORIDA
We Mean Healthy Business

(Fig. 10–1) This ad makes no more sense to the typical senior than "Yes, we have no bananas." In the 21st century, advertisers will unquestionably draw on a pool of experienced senior advertising writers and artists to create ads not only aimed at the biggest consumer group but instantly intelligible to that group. The next load of seniors will have even less patience than the one of today . . . and a considerably shorter attention span.

Greed, for years the winner in any motivational sweepstakes, may at last begin to flag, at least within this group. Status may well be more valuable to many than accruing more dollars, which means work.

Guilt? Only when it relates to generations yet to come, and even in the waning years of the 20th century guilt is losing steam. "You've earned it" washes out guilt like a stream of detergent from a hose.

Need for approval may have an interesting future, because this motivator is the cousin of exclusivity. Seniors have few contemporary idols on the level of Eleanor Roosevelt, Arthur Godfrey, or Dinah Shore. When comedian George Burns died in 1996 at age 100, he was admired and praised; but his value as a spokesman had long since waned. Unquestionably, though, new senior heroes will appear — military men, actors-turned-statesmen, women of achievement. They will be the touchstones of "need for approval" marketing in the year 2010.

Too, manners may reappear. It was not by accident that "Miss Manners," the syndicated columnist who writes on which spoon to use, why cereal boxes shouldn't be placed on the breakfast table, and other rules of etiquette, was featured on the cover of *Modern Maturity*. Toward the higher end of affluent seniorism, manners translate into need for approval. An entire industry could spring up around this development.

Which Medium Is the Message?

The race between television and direct response is heating up.

The United States Postal Service is gradually and grudgingly agreeing that, in the 21st century, without direct mail it will perish. First class mail has given way to faxes and e-mail and overnight courier. What's left are the two remaining contributors to postal health — periodicals and bulk mail. Coming up fast is a factor that was almost forgotten in the 1970–1995 period: parcel post.

Other countries were courting mailers as early as 1985. Some post offices have been sponsoring direct marketing events for years. First as an exhibitor at Direct Marketing Association conferences and then as an active participant, the U.S. Postal Service has indicated a desire for inclusion.

And seniors are the key.

Direct mail

Every major researcher agrees that people buy more by mail as they age. This may be because seniors have more time to read. Thus, longer letters have gradually replaced shorter letters in consumer mailings to seniors.

A disclaimer coming up, but the rule might be: Don't make a long story short. If you need the space to describe an unusual benefit or an unusual guarantee or an area of product supremacy, take the space. Some 16-page letters are pulling well, and this is now, in

No monthly plan premium.
No co-payments for prescriptions.
No co-payments for most AvMed doctor visits.

AvMed™
MEDICARE PLAN
Call us at 1-800-535-9355

(Fig. 10–2) A generation ago, no advertiser — including one whose message was aimed at the mature market — would use "naturalistic" models such as these. In the 21st century matching the image to those at whom the message is aimed will be mandatory, if the advertiser wants any penetration.

the pre-2010 era. The more reasons you give to respond, the more response you'll get.

One tempering factor: Letter length has to be tied to clarity. A supreme edict: When writing to seniors, subtlety *never* works best.

Now the disclaimer: Until demographers woke up to the reality of the senior citizen marketplace, assaults on this marketplace were spasmodic. Today we have an organized torrent. As the torrent becomes a major flood we face a double problem: the flood itself and reduced attention spans. So the ancient maxim will be more and more sensible each year: Test letter length, not only as a generic but in marketing individual products and services.

Television

Television is the other giant. In the late 1990s, those who study the medium say mornings are better when advertising to seniors; late night periods don't work as well for this group.

But late night has a peripheral pull, because the children of these seniors will be watching then. Will they buy insurance or sports equipment or travel for their parents, or at least alert them to availabilities? The possibility becomes more and more questionable as the 21st-century senior exhibits greater independence than did the previous generation. The image of a sad 45-year-old depositing a doddering parent in a nursing home can actually bring hate mail.

Telemarketing

How about that chimera, telemarketing?

The future is brighter than the present, because even though the seniors of the 1990s are telemarketing-resistant, their replacements don't reject a call as automatically. The rejection rate may go up, but one mitigating factor is the gradual sophistication of telemarketing from the "anything goes" days of 1970–1990.

Reluctance to make a toll-free call (even in the late 1990s some seniors doggedly refuse to acknowledge that toll-free numbers are indeed toll-free; and the various phone companies compound the problem by introducing new exchanges and by actually attaching a toll to some toll-free numbers) won't be a problem in the 21st century. These are people who grew up with toll-free numbers, have used them throughout their business careers, and anticipate their availability.

For outbound calls to this group, resistance still will be higher than to any other group; but resistance won't be as high as in the 1990s. Telemarketers, to stay in business, will refine their approaches, simplify them, smear them head to foot with sincerity and benefits, and build them around that magical word that overcomes skepticism: *rapport*.

The period of untrained telephone sales representatives (TSRs, in the trade) is just about over. The person who obviously is reading a script and obviously is struggling with the words in that script simply cannot compete and is best destined to a less-confrontational career.

Catalogs

Catalogs? Seniors are heavy catalog purchasers, and those in the catalog business wait eagerly for the ranks of seniors to swell. Already some catalogs are aimed at seniors only. By 2010, specialty catalogs that haven't cracked the wall of senior unfamiliarity with what they sell will have swarmed over that wall.

Technology already makes possible the production of mini-catalogs based on an individual's own areas of interest; so a single catalog company might send half a dozen different, *non-overlapping* catalogs to the same customer.

The Internet

The Internet? Who knows? At this writing, everyone is an expert on the Internet . . . and not only do predictions vary wildly; so do statements of who is surfing, which surfers are being converted to visitors, which visitors are being converted to buyers, and who is making money from Internet sites.

Seniors are the last to embrace this medium, but by 2010 someone aged 50 will have been born in 1960 and been 35 years old in 1995, the first great Internet year. The door to the Web will open wide as technology becomes simplified. So the Internet — the most spectacular circus of mini-marketplaces ever to appear — will take its place in marketing to seniors.

Already online services have "chat rooms" especially for seniors, and these rooms are loaded almost 24 hours a day. Seniors have a huge asset for Internet and online marketers: Of all groups, to them the pressures of time are the least significant.

Fig. 10-3 is a home page labeled, innocently, "Sources of Interest to Seniors." If an individual were to follow each of the options listed in just this one site, clicking on each link, it would be

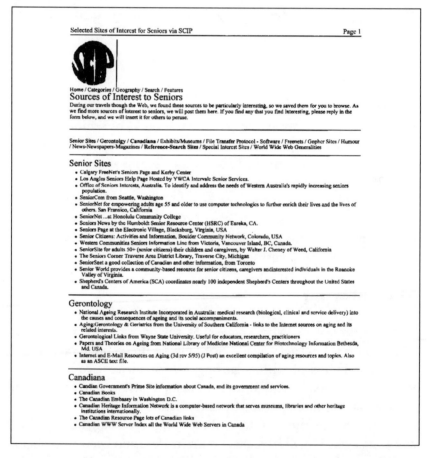

Selected Sites of Interest for Seniors via SCIP   Page 1

Home / Categories / Geography / Search / Features
Sources of Interest to Seniors
During our travels though the Web, we found these sources to be particularly interesting, so we saved them for you to browse. As we find more sources of interest to seniors, we will post them here. If you find any that you find interesting, please reply in the form below, and we will insert it for others to peruse.

Senior Sites / Gerontolgy / **Canadiana** / Exhibits/Museums / File Transfer Protocol - Software / Freenets / Gopher Sites / Humour / News-Newspapers-Magazines / **Reference-Search Sites** / Special Interest Sites / World Wide Web Generalities

Senior Sites
- Calgary FreeNet's Seniors Page and Kerby Center
- Los Angles Seniors Help Page Hosted by YWCA Intervale Senior Services.
- Office of Seniors Interests, Australia. To identify and address the needs of Western Australia's rapidly increasing seniors population.
- SeniorCom from Seattle, Washington
- SeniorNet for empowering adults age 55 and older to use computer technologies to further enrich their lives and the lives of others. San Fransico, California
- SeniorNet ...at Honolulu Community College
- Seniors News by the Humboldt Senior Resource Center (HSRC) of Eureka, CA.
- Seniors Page at the Electronic Village, Blacksburg, Virginia, USA
- Senior Citizens: Activities and Information, Boulder Community Network, Colorado, USA
- Western Communities Seniors Information Line from Victoria, Vancouver Island, BC, Canada.
- SeniorSite for adults 50+ (senior citizens) their children and caregivers, by Walter J. Cheney of Weed, California
- The Seniors Corner Traverse Area District Library, Traverse City, Michigan
- SeniorSnet a good collection of Canadian and other information, from Toronto
- Senior World provides a community-based resource for senior citizens, caregivers andinterested individuals in the Roanoke Valley of Virginia.
- Shepherd's Centers of America (SCA) coordinates nearly 100 independent Shepherd's Centers throughout the United States and Canada.

Gerontology
- National Ageing Research Institute Incorporated in Australia: medical research (biological, clinical and service delivery) into the causes and consequences of ageing and its social accompaniments.
- Aging:Gerontology & Geriatrics from the University of Southern California - links to the Internet sources on aging and its related interests.
- Gerontological Links from Wayne State University. Useful for educators, researchers, practitioners
- Papers and Theories on Ageing from National Library of Medicine National Center for Biotechnology Information Bethesda, Md. USA
- Internet and E-Mail Resources on Aging (3d rev 5/95) (J Post) an excellent compilation of aging resources and topics. Also as an ASCII text file.

Canadiana
- Candian Government's Prime Site information about Canada, and its government and services.
- Canadian Books
- The Canadian Embassy in Washington D.C.
- Canadian Heritage Information Network is a computer-based network that serves museums, libraries and other heritage institutions internationally.
- The Canadian Resource Page lots of Canadian links
- Canadian WWW Server Index all the World Wide Web Servers in Canada

(Fig. 10-3) This is the "home page" of one of many Internet sites aimed squarely at seniors. As familiarity with the medium increases and access becomes simple, senior domination of the Web is a definite possibility. The logic is tied to the size of the senior market.

- Champlain: Canadian Information Explorer a new service designed to make it possible to search for Canadian information on the Internet.
- KINDRED SPIRITS : OTHER CANADIAN WWW SITES collection of Canadian Sites by Jeff Lawrence
- NetLearn gives you access to a wealth of New Brunswick information to help you in various learning projects.
- New Brunswick Government Hot List
- Open Government Pilot undertaken by Industry Canada to provide greater access to government through information networks
- Proton Professional BBS good list of Bed & Breakfasts and Sailing info

News-Newspapers-Magazines

- Canadian based publications on-line
- Commercial Newspapers at Yahoo
- The Electronic News Stand
- Entertainment Magazines at Yahoo
- **News and Newspapers Online** Large list maintained by the Electronic Resources staff of Jackson Library, UNC-Greensboro.
- Daily News Links to **world-wide news sources**
- New York Times Syndicate - Computer News

Exhibits/Museums

- Web Acropol a virtual tour of Acropolis
- Canadian Museums from SeniorSnet
- **Guide to Museums and Cultural Resources** via The Natural History Museum of Los Angeles County
- Dead Sea Scrolls Exhibit
- Le Web Museum Fine Art from around the world
- Smithsonian Institution Museums an overview and links to their museums
- **Yahoo:Museums and Exhibits** large listing

File Transfer Protocol (FTP) - Share/FreeWare

- **The Oak Software Repository** - the definitive source for software.
- Query Interface to the PC Software Harvest Broker You can search the descriptions of more than 35,000 PC Software freeware distributions available from 6 major Internet archives.
- The Free Software /Shareware Shack
- Images, Icons and Flags Thousands of images, plus listings of more images....
- Walnut Creek CDROM Electronic Catalog

Freenets

- Blue Sky Community Network, Winnipeg, Manitoba
- International Freenets Listing courtesy of University of Wisconsin-Eau Claire
- Victoria Free-Net Home Page

Gopher Sites

A text only Internet protocol, pre-World Wide Web, but mature and HUGE!

- Gopher Servers world list from University of Minnesota
- Gopher Jewels offers a unique approach to gopher subject tree design and content
- Virtual Reference Desk The University of California Irvine (UCI)
- MBnet's Gopher Server
- University of Manitoba's Gopher Server

Humour

- Adrian's humor collection
- Confession Booth a cyber confessional, taken lightly
- **Humor** a collection from around the Internet

Reference/Search Sites

Large collections of reference information. Search engines allow you to enter a search word(s) in a text box and submit them. Returned will be links that apply to your search word

- **Search.com: excellent search tool; combines many search engines**
- EINet Galaxy a large reference source
- Global Network Navigator
- Internet Services List by Scott Yanoff
- The Whole Internet Catalogue
- The WWW Virtual Library
- Lycos search and index
- **Yahoo** excellent search tool and large index
- WebCrawler a major search engine
- WWW Search Engine Register **all the search engines on one page!** Australian National University

Special Interest Sites

- Boatnet Home Page
- The Genealogy Home Page Excellent genealogy reference and sources
- Joseph Luft's Philatelic Resources on the Web
- Packet Radio Home Page

World Wide Web Generalities

- All the Web Servers in the WORLD
- The World Wide Web Consortium has all the information about WWW developments

Please send comments, and updates to denesiuk@crm.mb.ca

impossible to complete the journey in one year. And that's just one site, of thousands available.

A lesson from the Internet

The Internet is the most visible example of what some might consider a counter-trend:

With each passing year, those entering the senior age group are less likely to think of themselves as seniors. They resent being corralled in an age-ghetto. So an increasing fragment of the senior market is becoming a segment rather than a fragment, and the segment may become a component. Constant study, not only of the marketplace as a whole but of the appeal of what *you* are selling, will help shape the nature of your sales appeals.

Not just possibly, but probably, marketers will employ two, three, or even half a dozen different approaches to reach different components of a complex market — a market homogenized in some respects and scattered in others.

How to Sell the 2010 Senior

Any prediction is based on probability, not fact. So, with the yolk of probability scrambled with the whites of opinion, here are some trends which should ripen between 1998 and 2010:

- Avoid scare tactics, except where such tactics relate to possible diminution of existing benefits. Scare tactics work less and less when selling commodities or lifestyle.
- Don't patronize. Seniors believe they deserve special benefits, but reminding them of this is an unwelcome patronizing intrusion by an outsider.
- Be straightforward in both copy and layout. Don't show off your massive vocabulary. Don't vary too far from noun-before-verb. Don't use puzzling layouts, as Fig. 10–1 does.
- Figure out a way to offer a discount. Seniors feel they've earned it, and the discount is light-years ahead of a "you've

earned it" cliché as a sales clincher. ("You've earned it," the utility infielder of approaches mentioned in chapter 6, may eventually phase out because of overuse. When you lean on this handy crutch, check competing marketers to be sure you aren't a "me too" user.)

- Use testimonials of people who parallel your targets, rather than celebrity endorsements. Whether you use testimonials or not, include case histories. Readers who find any kind of parallel with their own situation are considerably more likely to believe what you say.
- Avoid giddiness, "Golly gee willikers!" copy, and elephantine humor. These usually are a weak substitute for a genuine selling idea.
- Take the time and space to explain *why*. The straight "This is best" doesn't work on people who have spent a lifetime observing parallel claims by competing products.
- Assume the people you're contacting feel younger than they are.
- Reek of integrity. Except for the Clarity Commandment, of all the suggestions that can bring success in the 21st century, this is number one.
- The Clarity Commandment: When you choose words and phrases for force-communication, clarity is paramount. Don't let any other component of the communications mix interfere with it.

It's going to be an interesting time, isn't it? And, armed with awareness and recognition of what should work, for smart marketers it will be both interesting . . . and profitable.

About the Author

Herschell Gordon Lewis heads Communicomp, Plantation, Florida, U.S.A., a direct marketing creative source. He is a direct response writer and consultant, with clients throughout the world.

Among the organizations for which Mr. Lewis has written copy are the United Nations Children's Fund, Transamerica Insurance, Mutual Assurance, National General Insurance, Hearst Magazines, Cowles Business Media, Royal Copenhagen, Reader's Digest Travel Club, First Card, Consumers Union, Bellsouth, QVC Network, St. Jude Children's Research Hospital, Omaha Steaks, and the National Geographic Society. He also has written copy for many consumer and business catalogs, including Stark Bro's Nurseries, Black Box, and San Francisco Music Box Co.

Mr. Lewis's background includes more than 20 years as adjunct lecturer to graduate classes in Mass Communications, Roosevelt University, Chicago.

Among his books are *Copywriting Secrets and Tactics* (Dartnell); *Direct Marketing Strategies and Tactics* (Dartnell); *Big Profits from Small Budget Advertising* (Dartnell); *Herschell Gordon Lewis On the Art of Writing Copy* (Prentice-Hall); *Direct Mail Copy That Sells* (Prentice-Hall); *More Than You Ever Wanted to Know About Mail Order Advertising* (Prentice-Hall); *How to Make Your Advertising Twice as Effective at Half the Cost* (Bonus Books); *The Businessman's Guide to Advertising and Sales Promotion* (McGraw-Hill); *How to Write Powerful Fund Raising Letters* (Bonus Books); and *How to Handle Your Own Public Relations* (Nelson-Hall). He is the co-author of *Symbol of America: Norman Rockwell*. With his wife Margo he authored *Everybody's Guide to Plate Collecting*.

His most recent books are *Sales Letters that Sizzle* (National Textbook Company); *Open Me Now!* (Bonus Books); and (co-authored with Carol Nelson) *World's Greatest Direct Mail Sales Letters* (National Textbook Company).

Together with Ian Kennedy and Jerry Reitman, Mr. Lewis is producer of the recently-issued "100 Greatest Direct Response Television Commercials."

Mr. Lewis writes the monthly feature "Creative Strategies" for *Direct Marketing* Magazine and is the copy columnist for *Catalog Age*. He also writes "Copy Class" for the UK publication *Direct Marketing International*, "Better Letters" for *Selling* Magazine, and is the "Curmudgeon-at-Large" for *Direct*. He is a frequent contributor to *Fund Raising Management*. For years he conducted the copy workshop at the International Direct Marketing Symposium, Montreux, Switzerland, and he has appeared frequently at the Pan-Pacific Symposium in Sydney, Australia.

He also has addressed national direct marketing associations in countries such as Brazil, France, the U.K., New Zealand, Norway, Denmark, Sweden, Switzerland, Singapore, and South Africa ... and has been engaged to present copywriting seminars in many countries, including Mexico, Holland, Belgium, Germany, Hong Kong, and Indonesia. He is frequently called on to speak at meetings of the Direct Marketing Association, in the United States.

Mr. Lewis is a resident of Plantation, Florida (near Fort Lauderdale). He is a tennis player and scuba diver.

Index